DISCOURSE WARS IN GOTHAM-WEST

THE EDGE: CRITICAL STUDIES IN EDUCATIONAL THEORY

Series Editors   Joe L. Kincheloe, Peter McLaren, and Shirley Steinberg

Discourse Wars in Gotham-West

A Latino Immigrant Urban Tale of Resistance & Agency

Marc Pruyn

with a Preface by Peter McLaren

Westview Press

A Member of the Perseus Books Group

The Edge

Copyright © 1999 by Westview Press, A Member of the Perseus Books Group .

Published in 1999 in the United States of America by Westview Press, 5500 Central Avenue, Boulder, Colorado 80301-2877, and in the United Kingdom by Westview Press, 12 Hid's Copse Road, Cumnor Hill, Oxford OX2 9JJ

A CIP catalog record for this book is available from the Library of Congress.
ISBN 0-8133-9067-2

The paper used in this publication meets the requirements of the American National Standard for Permanence of Paper for Printed Library Materials Z39.48-1984.

10   9   8   7   6   5   4   3   2   1

To Amy M. Lam Wai Man,
Tallulah Moore and
Kaitlin Alaím Langston,
the three most incredible and
inspirational women I have ever known

Contents

Series Editors' Foreword

We are excited to include Marc Pruyn's *Discourse Wars in Gotham-West: A Latino Immigrant Urban Tale of Resistance & Agency* in our "Edge" Series at Westview. Making use of impressive literary skills, Pruyn asserts that the literature of critical pedagogy has not sufficiently addressed the forms of everyday talk that take place in critical classrooms. What specifically happens, he asks, when teachers set out to implement a critical pedagogy? In this context he quickly discovers that merely employing the language/jargon of a critical pedagogy by itself is not sufficient to accomplish critical goals. Indeed, there is no magic in criticalspeak—merely incanting it does not open the secret door to critical consciousness.

With these dynamics in mind, Pruyn seeks to explore the inner workings of if and how a critical pedagogy encourages students to gain a sense of agency. Influenced by a Freirean notion of agency, he concerns himself with the ways individuals come to see themselves in relation to other people and the socio-political world, how they gain the disposition and ability to change their environments in just and democratic ways. In the process of his research, Pruyn learns that such agency begins to develop in pedagogical situations that encourage students to think of themselves as literate and critical beings capable of transformative action. Thus, in *Discourse Wars in Gotham-West*, we gain a compelling glimpse of how critical pedagogy is (or is not) implemented in the classroom—in Pruyn's talented hands, the insight gained is profound.

A key to Pruyn's success in this task involves his understanding of discourse theory. Using this valuable tool, he asks what specific discursive practices work to promote or undermine critical pedagogical goals. The development of agency, he posits, is inseparable from the discursive features of the classroom. Disjunctions frequently occur between the formal curriculum of a critical classroom and the teacher's discursive positioning of students. This discursive positioning can clearly squash any agentive development promoted by the curriculum. Such dynamics become central to the success or failure of critical pedagogy. With these issues in mind, Pruyn focuses his attention on the *Siempre Adelante* ("Always Forward"), an organization developed to provide support to the Salvadoran, Guatemalan, and Mexican refugee communities of Los Angeles, and its critical education program. The research described in this book took place in this context. The *Siempre Adelante* educational program employed Freirean methods to promote Spanish literacy and English fluency to individuals in the refugee community. Pruyn focuses his attention on the work of three teachers and one group of students they all taught. In this educational context, he studies the interrelationship among the goals of the program, the pedagogical practices, the discursive positioning of students, and the changes discernible in student consciousness and action. As readers follow the social, political and educational dynamics delineated in this story, they gain important insights into connections between critical pedagogical theory and practice. Pruyn's work is a valuable addition to the literature of critical education. Students of critical pedagogy need to read this book for a variety of theoretical and practice-oriented reasons.

Joe L. Kincheloe,
Brooklyn College

Shirley R. Steinberg,
Adelphi University

Peter McLaren,
University of California, Los Angeles

Preface

Marc Pruyn first approached me about his study of a community-based, adult Spanish literacy project near downtown Los Angeles in the early summer of 1993. The city had spent a year recovering from a major uprising in South Central, and I had just arrived with a dusty and rust-splotched U-Haul, recovering from eight long years of teaching in a small and predominantly white and affluent Midwestern university. Moving to Los Angeles was the realization of a dream: it brought me closer to Latin America—both the Latin America that stood south of the U.S.-Mexican border, and the Latin America that resided within the United States, of which Los Angeles is the capital; my wife was able to continue her work in the movie industry (work that she had to abandon when we left Toronto, in our *madre patria*, Canada, in 1985); and it provided me with a challenging context for further developing my work in multicultural education, critical pedagogy, and Marxist theory. I was impressed with Marc from the very beginning. When he shared with me descriptions of his teaching career in a working class neighborhood of Central American refugees, and the study that he was planning to undertake at a community-based adult Spanish literacy project—*Siempre Adelante*—in the same neighborhood, I knew that this man "walked his talk," and that I had moved to the right place. Since Marc's appointment to the faculty of New Mexico State University, in Las Cruces, I have been fortunate to meet other students who share many of Marc's attributes: they are theoretically grounded; politically committed; ethically motivated; self-reflexive as well as self-critical; and filled with the passionate intensity necessary to make the world a better place. In my early days in "Los," Marc, in effect, became my teacher, as we moved through *las calles* and barrioscapes of my newly adopted city, listening to the *corridos* of Los Tigres del Norte, the hauntingly beautiful ballads of Selena, as well as *la quebradita, el conjunto*, and *la technobanda*.

Pruyn's *crónica* is very much the product of someone who lives within a *transfrontera* contact zone, among what José David

Saldívar calls "ethno-racialized cultures of displacement" (1997:7). The heteroglossic, *culturas híbridas*, and liminal spaces of Los Angeles had become, for Pruyn, sites of cultural and political contestation, where bi-national narratives of hope collided head-on with soul-wrenching narratives of despair; where nascent borderland subjectivities rubbed against the stubble of nationalist identities; where painful memories of Guatemala City and El Salvador were forgotten amidst the dizzying Saturday crowds at the Broadway Street *mercado*; where "the slashing rotors and booming loud speakers of LAPD helicopters" interrupt family gatherings after evening mass, spotlights criss-crossing the *patios* and the backyards like ghostly white shadows; where the *vendadores ambulantes* with their *elotes*, *raspados*, and *naranjas* of the East Side venture cautiously towards the outskirts of the fortress communities in the "*pinche*" Westside; where *los lavaplatos* and *domesticanas* working in the avant-garde hotels in the Sunset Plaza district line up in the evening for the long bus-ride home, watching in silence as the Hollywood elite cruise the palm-lined streets of Sunset Boulevard in stretch limousines.

Pruyn's work is one that stands in solidarity with the larger struggle for the liberation of the Americas. A critic of United States imperialism, Pruyn has worked with some of the Central American survivors of U.S.-supported dictatorships. He has seen the result of North American foreign policy initiatives aimed at solidifying the power of multi-national corporations and the ruling elite, initiatives often accompanied by covert acts carried out by the Central Intelligence Agency. As part of an important new generation of critical educational scholars, Pruyn sees the practice of research and scholarship as inextricably tied to a larger project of social and political transformation. In this work he has successfully brought together discourse analysis and classroom data both to criticize and advance the growing work that is being done in the field of critical pedagogy. His elaboration and combination of critical theory, neo-Marxist analysis, and critical discourse theories as they pertain to the development of critical student agency, is skillful and instructive. Especially within this present historical juncture of global capitalist expansion, Latinophobia, and physical assaults against immigrants south of *la línea*, Pruyn's works demands serious attention.

Building on insights from radical North and South American educators to the recent work of scholars engaged in socio-linguistic theory, Pruyn undertakes a sophisticated examination of how critical pedagogy works in both theory and practice in the lives of one group of students and their three teachers at *Siempre Adelante*. Serving Latina/o immigrants (predominantly Central American and Mexican) in a Central American community in Los Angeles, *Siempre Adelante* was inspired by the work of radical Bra-zilian educator Paulo Freire. This community-based organization sought to develop the academic competencies of students, as well as their sense of critical agency. Attentive to issues of ethnicity, gender, and class, Pruyn charts the possibilities of creating a counter-hegemonic discourse community in the classroom which nurtures the development of what he calls "critical student agency." Pruyn's analysis reveals that specific social practices on the part of students and teachers produced particular discourse communities in the classroom. These discourse communities, in turn, fostered or hindered the development of critical student agency.

Discourse Wars in Gotham-West is one of the few scholarly works on critical pedagogy that makes use of empirical data in the specific context of analyzing both academic and sociopolitical ar-ticulations of critical student agency and agentive growth. In this respect, Pruyn has begun to chart out a new *frontera* in the ongo-ing development and refinement of critical pedagogy. *Discourse Wars* is an excellent foundational text for novices of critical peda-gogy (such as teachers and graduate students), as well as for criti-calist researchers seeking a deeper and more nuanced under-standing of liberatory and democratic pedagogies put into prac-tice.

Peter McLaren,
University of California, Los Angeles

Reference

Saldívar, J. 1997. *Border Matters: Remapping American Cultural Studies.* Berkeley: University of California Press.

Acknowledgments

Many loving family members, wise mentors & teachers, supportive colleagues & co-workers and enthusiastic students, over many years, have assisted me—directly and indirectly—in bringing this work to fruition. While I wrote the pages you are about to read (and understand that any shortcomings this text may have are my responsibility alone), I hope you hear not only my voice, but also the voices, *deseos*, imaginations and whispers of all those who have helped to shape me (intellectually and personally) and to shape this text; for many stand quietly and with much dignity by my side.

First, I would like to thank my family, especially Amy M. Lam Wai Man, my partner, Tallulah Moore, my mom, and Kaitlin Alaím Langston, my daughter. Without their encouragement and assistance, this book would *literally* not have been possible. I would also like to thank Condy Lam, Baco Lam, Lan Heung Lam, Kwong Sun Lam, Leonard Golding Pruyn, Earl Moore and David Houlden. All of these kind and generous people gave me the love, guidance and support that made this work possible.

Second, I would like to express my gratitude to those I consider my mentors and teachers—some formal, some informal, some who I worked with personally, some who inspired me solely through their writings and actions—Peter McLaren, Kris G. Gutierrez, Carlos Alberto Torres, Elinor Ochs, Gustavo Enrique Fischman, Max Contreras, Sylvina Rubenstein, Philip Gonzales, Joe Kincheloe, Shirley Steinberg, Antonia Darder, Donaldo Macedo, Kathleen Weiler, Daniela Comaleras, Paulo Freire and Antonio Gramsci. It has been one of my greatest pleasures to learn from these fine intellectuals and social activists.

Third, I would like to thank those, beyond my editor, who spent many hours proof-reading and editing my manuscript: Amy M. Lam Wai Man, Gary Ivory, Luis Huerta and Marsha Cline. They assisted greatly in making this a clearer and more fluid text.

Fourth, I would like to convey my appreciation to colleagues and co-workers from New Mexico State University (NMSU), the

University of California, Los Angeles, Los Angeles Unified School District (LAUSD) and United Teachers-Los Angeles. Colleagues Rudolfo Chávez Chávez, Hermán García, Betsy Cahill, Leví Roberto Gallegos, James O'Donnell, Christine Clark, Rachel Theilheimer, Marah DeMeule, Mark Allan, Tara Gray, Joanne Larson, Steven Kowalski, Alberto Valdivia, Helen Bernstein, Debbie Michels, Kuaku Annor, Cristina Martin, Elena Zelaya, Douglas Clark, Claire Rexon and Patricia Martinez-Miller provided much guidance and *apoyo*. Co-workers Grace Martinez, Barbara Franco, Sergio Ruiz, Michael Reyes, Nancy Bustillos, Christine Hurtley and Nan Yang also lent much support. I am a better person for having worked with these dear *colegas* and *compañeros*.

Fifth, my students—both within the LAUSD and at NMSU—deserve special acknowledgment. For, in a very real sense, it was the thousands of elementary students I had the pleasure of working with in Los Angeles for the better part of a decade (both in and outside of my classroom), and their families, that inspired me to strive to become a critical intellectual and activist. This tradition has continued with many fine students at New Mexico State, including Jeanne Escudero, Laurel Partin, Vernalynn Andrews, James Smolinski, Rosa Mariscal, Liz Skramstad, Carole Newman, Lori Gibson, Cruzita Sánchez, Mandy Cordóva, Juan Manuel Pérez, Stephanie Mondragón, Katie Burk, Blanca Merewether, LaDonna House and Juan José Uribe. I truly believe that these "students-teachers" have made me a better "teacher-student."

Sixth, I would be remiss if I did not thank my editor, Catherine Murphy, and the other talented and supportive production staff at Westview press, including Sarah Warner, Jane Raese, Michelle Trader, Todd Tobias and Cindy White. Their editorial and publishing skills made this process smooth and worry-free.

Seventh, and finally, I would like to thank the strong, determined and heroic teachers and students from *Siempre Adelante*. May we all learn from you.

Gracias a todos ustedes, buenos amigos.

Marc Pruyn
Las Cruces, New Mexico
May 1998

DISCOURSE WARS IN GOTHAM-WEST

1

Studying Critical Student Agency

*The best place to view Los Angeles of the next millennium is from the ruins
of its alternative future. Standing on the sturdy cobblestone foundations of
the General Assembly Hall of the Socialist city of Llano del Río—Open
Shop Los Angeles's utopian antipode—you can sometimes watch the Space
Shuttle in its elegant final descent towards Rogers Dry Lake.*

—Mike Davis (1990:3)

Six-year-old Joana, one of my many Salvadoran students, told me
one morning that she was having trouble sleeping. She was being
plagued by recurring nightmares of the aerial bombings she and her
family had endured in El Salvador at the hands of the U.S.-
backed and armed dictatorship every time a helicopter would
pass over her working class neighborhood near downtown Los
Angeles. Joana and a good number of her classmates were rou-
tinely haunted by these and other similarly horrifying memories of
their lives prior to moving to *El Pueblo de Nuestra Señora de Los Angeles.* However, these experiences were not exclusively to be had in
my students' Latin American homelands. Other memories were
added to their mental scrap books as these and thousands of
other families were forced to make the trip from Central America
or Mexico, as political and economic refugees, to Gotham-West, a
city of some 13 million known more for its "streets of gold," palm
trees, plentiful beaches carefully guarded by young men and
women with exquisitely sculpted bodies, and movie studios, than
its poverty, overcrowdedness, smog, siege mentality police, and
general postmodern *malaise.*

To get to this paradise, these families had to depend on often
unscrupulous *coyotes* and pass through the barbed-wired and so-
dium-arc-lit "no man's land" occupied and patrolled by frequently vicious and abusive U.S. border agents. Once in the City

of the Angels, these immigrants began to face the realities of this border megalopolis: jobs were harder to find and paid much less than at first imagined, child care (beyond the K-12 public school system) was non-existent or too costly, landlords cared less about tenant safety and insect or vermin infestation than their monthly "take," and constant hounding by the Immigration and Naturalization Service (INS) and Proposition 187-emboldened European American racists (self-appointed keepers of the gates)[1] was commonplace. These were the memories and fears that worked at the imaginations and psyches of my students and their families.

And these student and community preoccupations did not stop at our classroom door at eight in the morning and patiently wait in the hall for the clock to strike three. They did not reside only in the worried minds of students as they tried to sleep through the noise produced by the slashing rotors and booming loud speakers of LAPD helicopters, or in the furrowed brows of their parents over the dinner table. They came inside our classroom. They were with my students as they tried to work their way through boring, irrelevant basal readers filled with stories about middle class, European American families in green and unpolluted Connecticut suburbs. They were with their parents as they listened patiently and respectfully during parent/teacher conferences while this young *güero* tried to explain to them how their child was academically progressing.

So, as I began my nine year teaching career working in this refugee neighborhood—the same neighborhood, and among the same people, where I would eventually conduct the study that is the focus of this book—I was driven to find a pedagogy that would assist me in struggling collectively with students and parents to make positive and substantive educational, political and economic changes in their lives in Gotham-by-the-sea. The U.S./IMF/World Bank policies that drove them from their homes in Latin American were no good. Their lives in Los Angeles— although they almost never overtly complained about them—were not lives, it seemed to me, steeped in social justice. And the pedagogy I was being asked to use, and the content I was being asked to teach in my classroom, were embarrassingly irrelevant.

I wanted to act to change these conditions. I knew that there must be better ways to teach. I knew that there must be better ways to act in social and political solidarity with this community; better ways to address and ameliorate some of the serious difficulties they, and all of us, faced.

Colleagues who found themselves in similar circumstances encouraged me to investigate the work of radical Brazilian educator, Paulo Freire. In particular, I was advised to read his hallmark work, *Pedagogy of the Oppressed* (1970). Freire's pedagogy, known in the educational literature as "critical pedagogy," theorized that teaching should foster both academic growth and critical awareness on the part of students. Freire's philosophy of education—as well as that of North American critical pedagogical theorists such as Peter McLaren (1986, 1989, 1995), Kathleen Weiler (1988, 1991, 1997), Henry Giroux (1984, 1992, 1994), Antonia Darder (1991, 1995a, 1995b), Joe Kincheloe (1990, 1993) and Michael Apple (1979, 1982, 1993)—helped my work with these primary grade students, their parents, and the larger community, become more meaningful and relevant.

My pedagogy, and its philosophical and political/cultural grounding, matured. The critical rumblings stirred to life from my early readings of these and other radical social theorists also led me to pursue the graduate studies that ultimately led me to my current occupation as an assistant professor in the Chihuahuan borderlands of Southern New Mexico.

As I began reviewing the work of Freire and other educational criticalists, my primary goal was to understand how critical pedagogy could be successfully implemented in classrooms and other educational settings. How had critical pedagogy been implemented across different educational contexts? Had it been successful in encouraging students to become more self-reflective about their own lives and the larger society? Had it invited students to take more of an active role in confronting obstacles in their lives? How, and in what ways, had critical pedagogy encouraged oppositional or counter-hegemonic forms of student action and agency?

As my studies continued, I discovered a significant body of research which elaborated attempts at employing Freirean pedagogy in Latin America, North America, Asia, Africa and elsewhere. This collective body of research described, in broad terms, the often positive results of implementing Freirean-based pedagogy in diverse geopolitical settings. For example, many attempts at Freirean education have resulted in increased levels of literacy and more political awareness and activity on the part of students.[2]

However, this literature often failed to elaborate on what kinds of face-to-face talk were being used in these classrooms; that is, what the specific discursive classroom practices were that contributed to the success or failure of such programs. Although the development of critical analytical skills on the part of students, and a propensity to take action based upon these analyses—an aspect of what I will later elaborate as "critical student agency"—was the goal of these programs, it was difficult to discern from the case studies *how* this was specifically fostered and developed, and, maybe even more importantly, how it came into existence in the course of everyday classroom practices.

This study is an attempt to look at just this issue. In this research, I explore how one group of adult students demonstrated, or failed to demonstrate, a propensity toward critical student agency. These students were members of an adult Spanish literacy classroom ostensibly driven by Freirean/critical pedagogical and philosophical goals in the same neighborhood where I taught as a teacher for almost a decade—several, actually, were parents of youngsters at my elementary school.

Before moving on to the next section, however, a question begs asking—and answering! What exactly do I mean by "critical student agency"? To answer this question, we must first come to grips with the notion of "agency." While there are many different ways to understand and make more concrete the concept of "agency," I define it in the following way: purposeful action taken by an individual, or group of individuals, in order to bring about change. Understood from a Gramscian perspective (1971), agency can be seen as purposeful action taken by an individual, or group of individuals, to facilitate the creation of *counter-hegemonic practices* and institutions (i.e., actions directed against any given society's cultural and political normative practices). I use the term *"critical student agency"* to refer to purposeful action taken by a student, or group of students, to facilitate the creation of counter-hegemonic *pedagogical* (i.e., educational) practices. The central focus of Chapter 2 will be to elaborate this definition in more detail through an examination of the relevant literature.

The Challenge and a Radical Solution

Contemporary public schools in Los Angeles, or in any other major North American urban center, face a wide array of problems which underscore the need for more liberatory and democratic forms of pedagogical practice that center around issues of social justice. The changing demographics of Southern Californian schools in particular have documented a growth of largely immigrant, non-English speaking, economically disenfranchised and politically disempowered students and their families (Darder, Ingle & Cox 1993). Yet the schools in Los Angeles are not fully prepared to meet the academic and linguistic needs these students bring with them (Los Angeles Unified School District 1990; Oakes 1985)—and the recent passage of the anti-bilingual education Proposition 227 (the so-called, "English for the Children" Initiative) in California only makes this situation worse.

According to some, schools are even *less* prepared to address students' personal and sociopolitical needs (Darder, Ingle & Cox 1993; Macedo 1993; McLaren 1994b). Underpaid teachers in over-crowded urban classrooms do not necessarily make connections themselves, or foster connected understandings among their students, between the book learning embodied in the "word" and the life learning we all bring with us to classrooms from our experiences in the "world" (Freire & Macedo 1987). And, unfortunately, the type of pedagogy this culminating century will most be remembered for—except for a few notable, yet peripheral, radical counter-movements—will be Fordist/industrialist approaches that would have us run schools and classrooms as factory assembly lines where students' minds are objectively and discretely constructed at specific work stations over time by automaton teachers who have access to "true" and "correct" facts in all their Enlightenment glory. This approach arguably reached its peak during the Reagan/Bush 1980s with moves toward "teacher proof" curricula and "de-skilling" of pedagogues. Given this, it is no wonder that teachers are not encouraged to make central in their pedagogy connections among learning, identity and agency (action taking).

Freirean pedagogies, however, *do* emphasize these relationships by focusing primarily on the link between students' reading the word (academic literacies and other competencies) and their reading the world (critiquing and understanding their various real life experiences). Freirean pedagogical theory (Freire 1970, 1985, 1994; Freire & Macedo 1998) puts at the center of the educational endeavor the development of academic competencies, critical awareness, analytical skills *and* agency. This theory posits that to be successful in achieving self and social empowerment, the development of academic skills, critical awareness and agentive attitudes are inseparable. As students are encouraged to see themselves as literate and critical analysts and actors—and are validated as such through their experiences inside and outside of classrooms—they develop positive self-images and begin to take academic, cultural and political actions as agentive human beings.

Yet little of the existing research examines how students *specifically* develop such critical forms of agency through classroom talk and gesture (i.e., discourse), or the specific outcomes of such development. Notably absent from this literature are discussions about the formation of critical student agency at the discursive level with data from classrooms. Additionally, few studies to date have examined the discursive practices of the classroom at the *micro*-interactional level of classroom life. I believe this approach to examining pedagogical interaction is key in that the function of agency in the classroom is closely tied to the social and discursive practices *of* the classroom.

To advance the project of Freirean/critical pedagogy, to show its viability as a radical and democratic alternative, especially during these politically and pedagogically challenging and conservative times, it is not only useful, but *necessary* to undertake just such forms of analysis. Through studies that identify what types of social interactions have encouraged critical growth among students in Freirean-oriented classrooms, we can better understand how critical student *agency* comes into existence. And, further, we can demonstrate when and how this type of pedagogical practice has been successful.

As McLaren suggests (1997), we as criticalists, and those who would seek to further the goal of social justice through education, need to be more self-reflective. We need to look at what we have been able to accomplish, and what we have *not* been able to accomplish. This self-examination needs to begin with a critique of actual attempts at Freirean/critical practice in various formal and informal educational settings: from Nicaragua's National Literacy Crusade of 1981 to daily classroom practices in Chicago's Pedro Albizu Campos Puerto Rican High School, from the grand scale of Myles Horton's Highlander Folk School in the Appalachian mountains to the modest Freirean-inspired Spanish adult literacy classroom in Los Angeles that was the focus of this study.

Our goal should not be to coldly analyze what has worked and what has not and then provide a "blueprint" for radical and progressive teachers to follow; Freire specifically cautions against this. But rather, our goal should be to show how we as radical educators can develop more successful ways of teaching and learning, ways consistent with the theories we evoke, to advance the critical agenda of student/teacher and teacher/student co-empowerment. And this desire for critical self-reflection and stock-taking, for self-analysis and the need for deeper understandings of what can make our approaches successful or unsuccessful in *real educational situations*, is what drove the study presented in this book.

This Study

I hope that the research described here will assist those of us interested in advancing radical and transformative forms of pedagogy to more deeply and fully understand how these pedagogies are, and can or could be, enacted discursively in specific educational settings. In this book, I examine an attempt at Freirean-inspired practice in one adult literacy classroom in order to understand how such pedagogical practices operate *in situ*. In formulating this study, I wanted to see how students' views of their own potential agency were constructed, and what specific discursive practices hindered or facilitated that construction. The central research question guiding this study was: What forms of social practice foster, or inhibit, the development of student critical agency in this classroom?

Because critical student agency is the desired outcome of Freirean-oriented education, my study focused on examining this construct. I hypothesized that critical student agency would be fostered when students were discursively positioned, by themselves and by the teacher, as active social subjects, and, alternatively, hindered when students were positioned through the discursive social practices of the classroom as *passive social subjects* (or "objects"). This investigation was designed to answer the question above and to test this hypothesis. The study was conducted within the context of an adult Spanish literacy classroom located within a working class Latino neighborhood of recent immigrants to Los Angeles. The classroom consisted of approximately six students (the number in actual attendance would vary over time), and was situated within a larger community-based, Freirean-inspired[3] English-as-a-second-language (ESL) and Spanish literacy project. The "subjects" of the study were one group of intermediate Spanish literacy students, and the three individuals—Guillermo, Daisy and Nadia—who served as their teachers over a thirteen month period.

The Organization of This Book

This book is organized into seven chapters. Chapter 2, "Building the Case for Critical Student Agency: Neo-Marxism, Poststructuralism, Critical Pedagogy and Discourse," will elaborate the theoretical framework that informs this study of the forms of social practice that foster or inhibit the development of critical student agency. The chapter will begin with a discussion of the notion of "agency" through the work of a number of major theorists for whom the concept has been of central import, beginning with the work of Antonio Gramsci (1971). The construct of agency will be further elaborated through an examination of the work of Michel Foucault (1977a, 1977b) and several poststructuralist thinkers (Derrida 1973, 1981; Laclau & Mouffe 1985; Lyotard 1984, 1989). This section will continue with an extended elaboration of the ideas of the most noted theorists working in the critical *pedagogical* tradition, and their contributions to the debate on agency (Apple 1979, 1986; Darder 1991, 1992; Giroux 1988, 1992; Giroux & McLaren 1994; Kincheloe 1991, 1993; McLaren 1986, 1989, 1995; Weiler 1988, 1997), with a particular focus on the work of Paulo Freire (1970, 1985, 1993) and Peter McLaren (1986, 1989, 1994a, 1997). The discussion of this study's orienting framework will conclude by focusing on the role of discourse in the production of student critical agency (Fairclough 1992a; Foucault 1977a, 1980; Gee 1990; Gutierrez, Stone & Larson, In Press; Ochs 1993), and the usefulness of "critical discourse analysis" in uncovering that production (Fairclough 1992a, 1992b; Gee 1990). Additionally, what the existing literature has to say about other studies that have examined similar issues will be reviewed and critiqued. In so doing, I will argue for the importance of this study in better understanding how critical student agency is fostered or hindered in daily classroom discourse.

The design and conceptualization of this qualitative research study will be detailed in Chapter 3, "Contextualizing the Study *en la Vida Cotidiana.*" In this chapter, the methods I used to analyze and uncover specific social and discursive patterns that either fostered or inhibited the development of critical student agency will be detailed. Additionally, Chapter 3 will include a description of the ESL/Spanish literacy program that constituted the research site, the types of data that were collected and the data collection methods that were used. The unit of analysis employed in organizing and selecting representative samples from the data, and the coding system that aided in both data organization, sampling and analysis, will be also discussed. Further, both the insights that I gained from a previous pilot study, and the challenges of this current study, will be highlighted.

Chapters 4, 5 and 6 comprise the study's data chapters. Because the discursive practices during literacy instruction under each of the three teachers were so distinct, each classroom[4] will be presented as its own "case," and then compared and contrasted to the others in order to understand the role and development (or lack thereof) of critical student agency in each setting. In this way, the relationships between the discursive practices of each classroom and critical student agency will be elaborated, problematized and discussed.

In Chapter 4, "Accepting the Word and the World: Accommodating Hegemony," findings from the classroom of Guillermo Linares and his students will be presented. This chapter discusses how the "hegemonic discourse community"[5] that Guillermo and his students co-constructed limited the development of critical student agency in their classroom.

Chapter 5, "Reading the Word through the World: Construct-ing a Counter-Hegemony," will present the findings from Daisy Contreras' classroom as she worked in very different ways with basically the same group of students. The findings from this class-room will illustrate how the students and teacher co-constructed, in this instance, a "*counter*-hegemonic discourse community," and consequently were able to foster critical student academic and so-ciopolitical agency.

Chapter 6, "Creating the World through the Word: Practicing Counter-Hegemony," as in the previous two chapters, will consist of the presentation of findings—this time, from the classroom of Nadia Monterey and her students—of the forms of social practice that fostered or inhibited the development of student agency. It will be shown how, in this classroom, the *students* (with a notice-able lack of participation on the part of the teacher) co-constructed a learning community that was alternately comprised of "hegemonic" and "counter-hegemonic" discourse. The data and discussion in this chapter will demonstrate how this community, despite its lack of hegemonic/counter-hegemonic fixity, continued to foster critical agency among its students, especially on the aca-demic plane.

Finally, Chapter 7, "Implications for Real Life: Critical Peda-gogy and Student Agency," will relate the study's findings back to the statement of the problem. How did the findings address the research problem? How did this study help us understand the de-velopment of critical student agency? Did the findings sufficiently examine how students develop agentive orientations at discursive levels? What future research in this area might prove useful? Ad-ditionally, this chapter will explore one of the most important questions of all, and one of the hardest to answer: So what? What real contribution has this study made to the field critical theory and pedagogy? To critical pedagogical researchers? To critical practitioners? Has it extended the debate on human agency?

Notes

1. In one case, soon after the passage of Proposition 187—which would have denied social benefits, including the right to a public edu-cation, to undocumented immigrants and their children (even if born in the United States)—two young Latinas were questioned about their

immigration/citizenship status by a European American counter worker at a fast food restaurant before he would serve them during their high school lunch break. Luckily, Proposition 187, after years of legal wrangling, has just recently been struck down in its entirety by the courts; this as Proposition 227 is in its ascendancy!

2. See Arnove 1981; Lappé & Medea 1986; Puiggrós 1983, 1986; Torres 1990, 1991; and the section "Freirean Pedagogical Theory: Towards The Development of a Critical Student Agency," in Chapter 2, below.

3. Through interviews with the directors of the project, as well as through ethnographic observation during teacher training sessions and document analysis, I came to understand that while situated within the larger theoretical/pedagogical camp of what North Americans call "critical pedagogy" and Latin Americans call "popular education"—of which there are many varieties—this project was Freirean in theoretical orientation (see Fischman 1994, 1998; La Belle 1986; Puiggrós 1983, 1986; and Torres 1990, 1991).

4. There was one group of students and three different teachers; i.e., three different "classrooms."

5. I am using the term "hegemonic discourse community," in terms of this study, to refer to a community of learners whose "Discourse" supports hegemonic pedagogical practices. By "Discourse" I mean teachers' and students' ways of speaking, writing, behaving, thinking, valuing, interacting and feeling; in other words, their "saying-doing-thinking-feeling-valuing" systems (see Gee 1990: xv-xx). Also, refer to the discussion in the section, "A Focus on Discourse: Searching For Agency in Everyday Practices and Talk," at the end of Chapter 2, below.

References

Apple, M. 1979. *Ideology and Curriculum*. New York: Routledge.

_____ . 1982. *Education and Power*. London: Routledge.

_____ . 1986. *Teachers and Texts: A Political Economy of Class and Gender Relations in Education*. New York: Routledge.

_____ . 1993. *Official Knowledge: Democratic Education in a Conservative Age*. New York: Routledge.

Arnove, R. June, 1981. "The Nicaraguan Literacy Crusade of 1980." *Phi Delta Kappan* 702-708.

Darder, A. 1991. *Culture and Power in the Classroom: A Critical Foundation for Bicultural Education*. Westport: Bergin & Garvey.

_____ . 1992. "Book review of *Pedagogy of the Oppressed*." *The Nation* 255: 301.

_____ . 1995a, ed. *Culture and Difference: Critical Perspectives on the Bicultural Experience in the United States.* Westport: Bergin & Garvey.

_____ . 1995b, ed. *Bicultural Studies in Education: Transgressive Discourses of Resistance and Possibility.* Claremont: Institute for Education in Transformation.

Darder, A., Ingle, Y., Cox, B. 1993. *The Policies and the Promise: The Public Schools of Latino Children.* Claremont: The Tomás Rivera Center.

Davis, M. 1990. *City of Quartz: Excavating the Future in Los Angeles.* New York: Vintage Books.

Derrida, J. 1973. *Speech and Phenomena, and Other Essays on Husserl's Theory of Signs.* Evanston: Northwest University Press.

_____ . 1981. *Positions.* Chicago: University of Chicago Press.

Fairclough, N. 1992a. *Discourse and Social Change.* Cambridge: Polity.

_____ . 1992b, ed. *Critical Language Awareness.* New York: Longman.

Fischman, G. 1994. "Schooling in Argentina in the 1990s: Is There Any Room Left for Popular Education and Critical Pedagogy?" Paper presented at the 1994 Meeting of the Comparative and International Education Society. San Diego, California.

_____ . 1998. "Donkeys and Superteachers: Structural Adjustment and Popular Education in Latin America." *International Review of Education* 42: 177-199.

Foucault, M. 1977a. *Discipline and Punish: The Birth of the Prison.* Sheridan, A., trans. New York: Pantheon.

_____ . 1977b. *The History of Sexuality, Volume I.* Hurley, R., trans. New York: Pantheon.

_____ . 1980. *Power/Knowledge: Selected Interviews and Other Writings.* Gordon, C., ed. New York: Pantheon.

Freire, P. 1970. *Pedagogy of the Oppressed.* Rámos, M., trans. New York: Continuum.

_____ . 1985. *Politics of Education.* South Hadley: Bergin & Garvey.

_____ . 1993. *Education for Critical Consciousness.* New York: Continuum.

_____ . 1994. *Pedagogy of Hope: Reliving Pedagogy of the Oppressed.* New York: Continuum.

Freire, P. and Macedo, D. 1987. *Literacy: Reading the Word and the World.* Massachusetts: Bergin & Garvey.

Freire, P. and Macedo, D. 1998. *Teachers as Cultural Workers: Letters for Those Who Dare Teach.* Boulder: Westview.

Gee, J. 1990. *Social Linguistics and Literacies: Ideology and Discourses.* London: Falmer.

Giroux, H. 1984. "Ideology, Agency, and the Process of Schooling." In Barton, L. and Walker, S., eds. *Social Crisis and Educational Research*. London: Croom & Helm.

_____. 1988. *Teachers as Intellectuals: Toward a Critical Pedagogy of Learning*. Westport: Bergin & Garvey.

_____. 1992. *Border Crossings: Cultural Workers and the Politics of Education*. New York: Routledge.

_____. 1994. *Disturbing Pleasures: Learning Popular Culture*. New York: Routledge.

Giroux, H. and McLaren, P. 1992. "Writing from the Margins: Geographies of Identity, Pedagogy, and Power." *Journal of Education* 174: 7-30.

Gramsci. A. 1971. *Selections from the Prison Notebooks*. Medea, Q. and Smith, N., eds. and trans. London: Lawrence & Wishart.

Gutierrez, K., Stone, L. and Larson, J. In Press. "Hypermediating in the Urban Classroom: When Scaffolding Becomes Sabotage in Narrative Activity." In Baker, C., Cook-Gumperz, J. and Luke, A., eds., *Literacy and Power*. Oxford: Blackwell.

Kincheloe, J. 1990. "Meta-Analysis, Memory and the Politics of the Past: Historical Method, Curriculum and Social Responsibility." *Social Science Record* 27: 31-39.

_____. 1991. "Educational Historiographical Meta-Analysis: Rethinking Methodology in the 1990s." *Qualitative Studies in Education* 4: 231-245.

_____. 1993. *Toward a Critical Politics of Teacher Thinking: Mapping the Postmodern*. Westport: Bergin & Garvey.

La Belle, T. J. 1986. *Non-formal Education in Latin America and the Caribbean: Stability, Reform, or Revolution?* New York: Praeger.

Laclau, E. and Mouffe, C. 1985. *Hegemony and Socialist Strategy: Towards a Radical Democratic Politics*. London: Verso.

Lappé, F. M. and Medea, B. 1986. *Nicaragua: Give Change a Chance*. San Francisco: Food First Books.

Los Angeles Unified School District. 1990. *The Children Can No Longer Wait! An Action Plan to End Low Achievement and Establish Educational Excellence*. Los Angeles: Los Angeles Unified School District.

Lyotard, J. 1984. "An Interview." *Theory, Culture, and Society* 5: 277-310.

_____. 1989. *The Lyotard Reader*. Benjamin, A., ed. London: Basil Blackwell.

Macedo, D. 1993. "Literacy for Stupidification: The Pedagogy of Big Lies." *Harvard Education Review* 63: 183-206.

McLaren, P. 1986. *Schooling as a Ritual Performance: Towards a Political Economy of Educational Symbols and Gestures.* London: Routledge.

———. 1989. *Life in Schools: An Introduction to Critical Pedagogy in the Foundations of Education.* New York: Longman.

———. 1994a. "Rasquachismo and Critical Pedagogy in the Age of Global Capitalism." Paper presented at the annual convention of the American Educational Research Association. New Orleans, Louisiana.

———. 1994b. "Multiculturalism and Moral Panic: Critical Pedagogy and the Promotion of Unsettling Literacies." *Voices* 3: 1-11.

———. 1995. *Critical Pedagogy and Predatory Culture: Oppositional Politics in a Postmodern Era.* London: Routledge.

———. 1997. *Revolutionary Multiculturalism: Pedagogies of Dissent for the New Millennium.* Boulder: Westview.

Oakes, J. 1985. *Keeping Track: How Schools Structure Inequality.* New Haven: Yale University Press.

Puiggrós, A. 1983. "Discuciónes y Tendencias en la Educación Popular Latino-Americana." *Nueva Antropología* 6: 15-39.

———. 1986. *La Educación Popular en America Latina, 2.* México, D.F.: Secretaría de Educación Pública.

Torres, C. A. 1990. *The Politics of Non-Formal Education in Latin America.* New York: Praeger.

———. 1991. "The State, Non-formal Education, and Socialism in Cuba, Nicaragua, and Grenada." *Comparative Education Review* 35: 110-130.

Weiler, K. 1988. *Women Teaching for Change: Gender, Class and Power.* South Hadley: Bergin & Garvey.

———. 1991. "Freire and a Feminist Pedagogy of Difference." *Harvard Educational Review* 61: 449-474.

———. 1997. "Reflections on Writing a History of Women Teachers." *Harvard Educational Review* 66: 635-657.

2

Building the Case for
Critical Student Agency:
Neo-Marxism, Poststructuralism,
Critical Pedagogy and Discourse

Today's globalized culture with its lifestylization grounded in consumption patterns provides an urgent backdrop for revisiting Gramsci...

—McLaren, Fischman, Serra & Antelo (1998:2)

The focus of this study is "critical student agency" and how its construction is fostered or hindered through classroom discourse. But what is critical student agency? In the first chapter it was defined as purposeful action taken by a student, or group of students, to facilitate the creation of counter-hegemonic pedagogical practices. But this definition needs to be more historically and theoretically fleshed-out. In beginning to do so, the more general concept of "agency" must first be scrutinized. We must address questions such as: What *is* agency? Does it even exist? Is agency possible? How is it more generally defined and understood? What forms does it take? What is agency's role in cultivating social change? Why, or how, do people change their material, social and personal conditions of existence through agency? Perhaps even more importantly, why is it that they often *do not*? What does agency look like in classrooms? Without conducting an exhaustive archeology of the term and concept, I will attempt to answer these questions by tracing the development of the notion of agency through the work of several major thinkers and schools of thought for whom agency has been a key concept.[1] In other words, I will not use this chapter as an opportunity to reproduce, critique and analyze *all* of the definitions, positions and arguments generated around the notion agency over the last several centuries; rather, I will draw on the ideas of several specific scholars, from different fields of social theoretical thought, in trying to construct a working definition of agency, as I understand it, in the context of this study.

The goal of the first three sections of this chapter will be to theoretically develop the notion of "critical student agency." In Section 1, "Gramsci: Agency through Counter-Hegemonic Action," the work of Italian communist Antonio Gramsci (1971) will be elaborated in order to provide a background and definition of "agency." Section 2, "Foucault and Poststructuralism: Positioning Subjects and Challenging Agency," will detail the work of French philosopher Michel Foucault (1977a, 1977b) and several leading theorists working within the poststructuralist tradition (Derrida 1981, 1994; Jean-François Lyotard 1984; and, Laclau & Mouffe 1985). I will describe how their work has simultaneously provided forms of analysis that help identify agency and has also challenged the notion of agency itself. The theoretical discussion of agency will conclude in Section 3, "Critical Pedagogical Theory: Agency In and Out of Classrooms," as the work of critical pedagogical theorists Paulo Freire (Freire 1970, 1985, 1997; Freire & Macedo 1998), Peter McLaren (1995, 1997), Kathleen Weiler (1988, 1991), Henry Giroux (1992), Antonia Darder (1991), Joe Kincheloe (1990, 1991) and Michael Apple (1982) will be presented. It is within this section that the journey from "agency" to "critical student agency" will theoretically conclude. (Analytically, however, this journey will just have begun.) Based on the work of these critical educational theorists, it will be show how the concept of "critical student agency" was constructed and operationalized for this study of one Freirean-inspired adult literacy classroom.

This chapter will continue with the section, "Freirean Pedagogical Practice: Striving for Agency, Creating Change," where attempts at critical pedagogical practice will be reviewed and critiqued. Research that is similar to my own will be examined in order to situate this study, and its unique contribution, within the field of critical pedagogy. The chapter will conclude with the section, "A Focus on Discourse: Searching for Agency in Everyday Practices and Talk," which will focus on how researchers have used discourse analysis to understand social processes in class-rooms, and how I intend to use "critical" discourse analysis in identifying the development of critical student agency in this study.

Gramsci: Agency Through Counter-Hegemonic Action

Antonio Gramsci, a founder of the Italian Communist Party, has generated much discussion in this century on the nature of social control and human agency through his theories of "hegemony" and "counter-hegemony." While vanquished to Mussolini's fascist prisons during the last eleven years of his life, he composed what would later become perhaps his most influential work, *The Prison Notebooks* (1971). These notebooks marked a major reinter-pretation of Marxism, especially in regard to cultural institutions and revolutionary organization. Gramsci expanded Marxism past its economic roots to include political, social and cultural theoreti-cal elements (Gramsci 1971; Holub 1992). While economics were still key, Gramsci brought new attention to the role culture plays in *maintaining* the economic order and its revolutionary potential for changing it (Gramsci 1971). Gramsci's primary contribution to the theory of agency was through this elaboration of "hegemony" and "counter-hegemony."

According to Gramsci, it is through *hegemony* that a society's cultural institutions reproduce and reinforce the economic sys-tem—building on Marx's notion of a cultural superstructure (the state, family, law, media, religion, schools, *et cetera*) that supports the economic infrastructure of capitalism (Marx 1963; Marx & Engels 1972). Morrow & Torres (1995) describe Gramsci's idea of hegemony as the "ideological predominance of bourgeois values and norms over the subordinate social classes...by moral and in-tellectual persuasion" (253). Schools, for example, as one of the many cultural tools of the bourgeoisie, can serve to cement the ex-isting economic/social order in place by presenting these cultural practices as "natural" and "normal." According to Gramsci, he-gemony—social and ideological control and domination—operates at the level of "consent" in "civil societies" (1971). Coercive force is brought to bear by the bourgeois state only as a last resort, when the dominant ideology enters a crisis. Darder (1991) summarizes Gramsci's theory of hegemony well when she states that (34-35):

> The theory of hegemony has emerged from a concern with the changing forms of domination that have developed in advanced industrial societies. With the rise of modern science and technology, social control has been exercised less through the use of physical deterrents and increasingly through the distribution of an elaborate system of norms and imperatives. Gramsci notes that—unlike fascist regimes, which control primarily through physically coercive forces and arbitrary rules and regulations—capitalist societies utilize forms of hegemonic control that function systematically by winning the consent of the subordinated to the authority of the dominant culture...Hegemony in American schools results, more specifically, from institutionalized social relations of power that are systematically asymmetrical, and therefore unequally privilege students from the dominant culture over students from subordinate cultures.

Gramsci's notion of hegemony provided a new way for social scientists and philosophers to think about the connectedness of economic and cultural institutions and systems. As Holub notes, armed with the analytical concept of hegemony, social scientists and researchers were now able to probe

> relations of power on a microstructural as well as on a macrostructural level. With this concept...[Gramsci] attempted to extend [examinations of] relations of power beyond the hierarchical relation of state and citizen...to other areas of society...[to] the practices of everyday life. (1992:196-197)

Through hegemonic processes in cultural institutions such as the press, church, families, political parties and schools, the dominant sectors of society (the capitalist class and its allies) control the popular sectors of society (the working class and its allies) through a combination of "consent" and "coercion" (Gramsci 1971). In understanding how hegemony is constituted and functions, we can begin to understand how its opposite, *counter*-hegemony, is constituted and functions. And it is through counter-hegemony that the idea of agency begins to figure prominently in this discussion.

It is through Gramsci's theorizing on the possibility of, and need for, a "counter-hegemony," that oppressive and hegemonic cultural institutions, and ways of understanding the world, can be transformed into sites of revolution and social change. Through counter-hegemony, Gramsci's focus turns to individual and group *agency*. He envisions the discovery and creation of "organic intellectuals" from within the working class who could begin questioning and challenging the vision of prevailing hegemonic culture among the masses. Within schools, this role would be filled by radical teachers. Through the work of an "historic bloc," a coalition of sectors of the working class and their sympathizers, a different way of viewing society and its institutions could be encouraged. This counter-vision, as developed by the organic intellectuals, and as advanced by the historic bloc, could eventually supplant the existing hegemony, or could serve as a cultural revolutionary movement in advance of political revolution. On one point Gramsci was clear, successful political revolution was not possible without cultural transformation. State apparatuses could be seized, but if they were not changed, and culturally reconceptualized beforehand, they would only serve to maintain the cultural logic of the previous social order after the revolution (1971).

By focusing on the transformational potential of individuals ("organic intellectuals" and "workers") and groups (the "historic bloc" and the "working class") through counter-hegemonic cultural agency, Gramsci theorized a major break with the modernist Enlightenment project of the time, and its grand "meta-narratives."[2] In particular, Gramsci formulated a theoretical alternative to the determinist Marxism of his era by allowing for, and theorizing, agency. In terms of the theoretical framework within which this study is grounded, it was through Gramsci's theories of hegemony and counter-hegemony that the modern debate on agency was begun.

No discussion of agency would be complete, however, without addressing "resistance." Continuing to follow the hegemony/counter-hegemony paradigm elaborated by Gramsci, "resistance" occurs when individuals demonstrate displeasure, or even act-out, against hegemonic structures, but without the goal of reconstituting those structures (1971). Some, however, see acts of resistance, which are often smaller in scale and more subtle than acts of agency, as just as transformative of dominant cultural practices as agentive acts. According to some feminist and critical postmodern theorists, for example, cultural practices of resistance do not always necessarily take the form of explicitly oppositional acts (McLaren 1995), but can still have great impact. For example, O'Hanlon (1988) claims that:

> Rejecting the view of resistance as deliberate political opposition, we should look for resistance of a different kind; dispersed in fields we do not conventionally associate with the political; residing sometimes in the evasion of norms or the failure to respect ruling standards of conscience and responsibility...From this perspective, even withdrawal from or simple indifference to the legitimating structures of the political, with their demand for recognition of the values and meanings which they incessantly manufacture, can be construed as a form of resistance. (222-223)

According to Gramsci, resistance is simply a matter of displaying signs of subaltern discontent rather than making conscious efforts at social change. Gramsci sees resistance as a largely unconscious act that needs to be replaced by agency to effectively develop counter-hegemonic structures (Gramsci 1971). Similarly, Willis (1977) has shown how undirected, uncoordinated and unstrategic efforts at resistance may even serve to reinforce hegemonic practices and forms of domination. In terms of this study, I posit that it is through taking agentive stances and actions that individuals begin to see themselves—although not necessarily using this lexicon—as potential socio-political actors, as "subjects of history" (Apple 1995:xiii) and "authors of their own lives" (Casey 1993 in Apple 1995:xiii). Through participation in agentive acts, individuals begin to recognize, and struggle against, attempts by hegemonic cultural institutions to position them as passive followers and conformists. Agency *supplants and extends* resistance as counter-hegemonic attitudes are fostered and spread through subjugated sectors and groups within society (Gramsci 1971).

In concluding this section on Gramsci and agency, it would be useful to restate and elaborate working definitions of "agency" and "critical student agency" that will be used throughout this study. While recognizing that there are many different ways to understand and operationalize "agency," I define it here as purposeful action taken by an individual, or group of individuals, in order to bring about change. Understood from a Gramscian perspective, agency could be seen as purposeful action taken by an individual, or group of individuals, to facilitate the creation of counter-hegemonic practices and institutions. Even more specifically, I will use the term "critical *student* agency" to refer to purposeful action taken by a student, or group of students, to facilitate the creation of counter-hegemonic pedagogical practices.

I will draw on the work of Foucault (1977a, 1977b), and a number of theorists working within the poststructuralist tradition (Derrida 1973, 1981, 1994; Lyotard 1984, 1989; Laclau & Mouffe 1985), in the following section, to marshal the theoretical tools that have helped me identify agency in practice in this study. Paradoxically, at the same time that the work of these theorists proves useful in understanding how agency is discursively (i.e., linguistically, culturally and gesturally) formed, it also represents a major theoretical challenge to the whole *notion* of agency.

Foucault and Poststructuralism: Positioning Subjects and Challenging Agency

Michel Foucault: Hegemony, Discipline and Power
Michel Foucault (1977a, 1977b) posits that human beings come to occupy the subject positions they do in the social world largely through "discipline." Discursive social, "regularized" and "naturalized" ways of being and behaving are imposed upon us from without by society's institutions, and eventually become internalized such that we begin policing ourselves, much in the same way Gramsci theorized the workings of hegemony. From a Foucauldian perspective, notes Zaretsky, "we are made into subjects from 'above,' e.g., in prisons, schools, and hospitals, but also from 'below,' e.g., through confessional or communicative practices such as psychoanalysis" (1994:10). We are formed, and form ourselves, as social subjects in different situations. Discipline eventually "works not from the outside but from within...at the level of detail...by...producing [individuals]...[E]xterior power gives way to an internal, productive power" (Foucault 1977a:203). Holub, commenting on the similarities between Gramscian and Foucauldian thought, notes:

> What Gramsci and Foucault share...is the notion that power and domination function in so far as those dominated consent to that domina-

tion...What Gramsci and Foucault also share is their understanding of the production of that consent. It is produced from within the systems and subsystems of social relations, in the interactions, in the microstructures that inform the practices of everyday life. (1992:199)

Where Gramsci and Foucault do not agree is in the areas of counter-hegemony, resistance and agency. Since Foucault holds that "power is everywhere local" (1977a), there is little room for agency. With a focus on our discursive production as social subjects from above and below (i.e., out of our direct control), Foucault theorizes little room for individual or group agency, or its potential to alter the hegemonic order. When there is not a specifically pinpointable and unified "enemy"[3] to struggle against, when power is always diffuse and ever-present, and when we ourselves are simultaneously involved in multiple power relationships such that we might at one moment be an "oppressor," and at another, "oppressed," how do we resist, or act agentively? And against whom?

Foucault posits that discourse[4] plays a pivotal role in how power relations are acted-out in our daily lives in the social world. He claims that after being discursively disciplined and watched by others, we begin to discipline and watch (regulate) ourselves. If we comply with the normalizing judgments of the dominant discourse, we are rewarded. If we go against them, we are either seen as "abnormal" or "deviant," ridiculed, and sometimes physically punished or incarcerated (Foucault 1977a, 1977b). It being easier to comply, we more often do so than not. Through these procedures, dominant ways of being and acting come to be seen as "natural" and "normal," and we continue to do them. Closely paralleling Gramsci's theory of hegemony (1971), this practice holds true not just for cultural institutions such as prisons and "madhouses," but also for factories, households, schools and hospitals.

Given Foucault's understandings of power and agency, resistance within existing structures of oppression just reinforces those structures. He posits that it might be better not to resist oppressive social structures at all, at least not from within them. Foucault contends that it might be more fruitful to "play" outside of existing structures, not complying with or accepting how others position us as social subjects (1977b).

While claiming not to be a poststructuralist himself (Miller 1993; Usher & Edwards 1994), many of Foucault's positions on power, resistance and agency are analogous to positions taken by poststructuralist theorists. The following section will detail the positions taken by several major poststructuralist thinkers on these same issues and how they relate to this study.

Poststructuralism: The Diffusion of Struggle and a Challenge to Agency

Poststructuralism positions itself against the encompassing and deterministic nature of the modernist Enlightenment project, and the meta-narratives that guide it. As McLaren notes, poststructuralism—as elaborated in the work of Jacques Derrida (1973, 1981, 1994), Jean-François Lyotard (1984, 1989), and Laclau & Mouffe (1985)—marks the "social rupturing of the unitary fixity and homogenizing logic of the grand narratives of Western European thought" (1995:13). From this point of view, there is more of a focus on local and diffuse power and struggles within discourse, as in Foucault's work, as opposed to large social changes and phenomena. From a poststructuralist standpoint, the social positions individuals are placed in through language, that is, their "subject positions," become the focus of inquiry and analysis. Notions such as "identity," "ego," "self" and even "class," "gender," and "race" become *de*-emphasized (Aronowitz 1994:228; Zaretsky 1994).

Poststructuralist theorists posit the existence of the "split" or "multiple" social subject. These subjects are produced and created as our lives are played-out in different discursive situations (Aronowitz 1994; Bauman 1988, 1995). The self is "hopelessly" and "creatively fragmented" into different subject positions that are produced through statements; that is, through discursive processes (Aronowitz 1994:9; Fariclough 1992a). And this is central, for in my estimation, we all *do* inhabit multiple, fragmented and oppressed "selves" as we live our lives out in different and constantly shifting contexts during these "late capitalist," postmodern and exploitative times. James Paul Gee (1990) talks about these multiple incarnations of self in terms of the different "Discourses" we all simultaneously and/or sequentially occupy.

Yet poststructuralism is not without its critics. The split, multiple, atomized and diffused nature of current social conditions hypothesized by poststructuralists (and others) is acknowledged and then problematized in the more recent work of McLaren :

> While some postmodernists adventitiously assert that identities can be fluidly recomposed, rearranged, and reinvented...I maintain that this is a shortsighted and dangerous argument. It would take more than an army of Jacques Lacans to help us rearrange and suture the fusillade of interpolations and subject positions at play in our daily lives. My assertion that the contents of particular cultural differences and discourses are not as important as how such differences are embedded in and related to the large social totality of economic, social, and political differences may strike some readers as extreme. Yet I think it is fundamentally necessary to stress this point...It is true that...poststructuralist and postmodern theories have greatly expanded how we understand the relationship between identity, language, and schooling; but all too often these discourses collapse into a dehistoricizing and self-congratulatory emphasis on articulating the specifics of ethnographic methodologies and the ideological virtues of asserting the importance of naming one's location as a complex discursive site. As essential as these theoretical forays have been, they often abuse their own insights by focusing on identity at the expense of power. (McLaren 1997:7; McLaren & Giroux[5] in McLaren 1997:17)

McLaren theorizes human beings as potential social actors, as agents, whose will is not subverted to the inescapable mandates of discourse:

> To know ourselves as *revolutionary agents* is more that the act of understanding who we are; it is the act of reinventing ourselves out of our overlapping cultural identifications and social practices so that we can relate them to the materiality of social life and the power relations that structure and sustain them. (emphasis mine, McLaren 1997: 12-13)

Criticisms notwithstanding, poststructuralist theory is helpful in understanding the processes by which we are externally and discursively placed in different subject positions; how we ourselves become complicit in this process; and how this can limit us. But what, then, about social action? What role is there for individual and collective action? This poststructuralist stance can be problematic when one considers the role, and social construction, of (student) agency. If identity, self, class, gender and race are no longer central issues in a project for social justice, because forms of oppression are hyper-localized, is there any possibility for individual or group agency? This is problematic.

Some, like "post-Marxist"/poststructuralists Laclau & Mouffe (1985), incorporate the counter-hegemony theorized by Gramsci into their poststructuralist framework, while at the same time criticizing Gramsci for having remained overly wedded, in their appraisal, to the determinism of classical structuralist Marxism. They claim Gramsci's work does not adequately deal with subjectivity, discourse or the decentered nature of power (Laclau & Mouffe 1985; Morrow & Torres 1995).[6] So they reinterpret and extend Gramsci into their *post*-Marxist politics of decentering. As Holub notes, in the work of Laclau & Mouffe, "Gramsci is interestingly enlisted in the struggle for a radical democracy poststructurally conceived" (1992:209).

Following the logic of Foucauldian and poststructuralist theory, agency could be reduced to enactments of internalized, discursively predetermined, unconscious scripts. McLaren agrees that there is a tendency among some poststructuralists to "dissolve agency" and to claim that "we are always already produced and finalized as subjects within discourse" (1995:73). These theories posit that we are positioned as subjects, but not how we can take *action* as historical social subjects; how we can act collectively and politically against very real oppressive structures such as capitalism, sexism, racism and homophobia. McLaren, Fischman, Serra & Antelo (1998), in critiquing Derrida's poststructuralist challenge to Marxism in "Specters of Marx" (1994), note:

> In this deconstruction as exorcism, Derrida disavows class struggle and establishes an international built on the unfinalizability of discourses and the impossibility of political co-ordination...Uninterested in class politics, Derrida forecloses the possibility of mounting a program of anti-capitalist struggle.
>
> Marx understood vividly in a way that Derrida does not that discourses always converge and pivot around objective labor practices and that global capitalism has a way of reshaping, re-infecting, and rearticulating dissent. (3)

As researchers and theorists interested in examining how students are formed as social agents, from my perspective, these poststructuralist ways of conceiving the social are not helpful. To elaborate and examine the forms of resistance and agency taken up by the students in this study, I found it important to draw more on the insights of Gramscian theory as previously presented, and critical pedagogical theory, as presented in the following section.

Yet, because poststructuralist theory is helpful in describing how processes of domination occur through discursive placement, we might be able to theorize how processes of *liberation* from oppression might also occur by these same means. Of particular interest is this notion of the placement of others, and self-placement, in various subject positions through discourse, and the ramifications of this placement. According to this poststructuralist theoretical position, we are produced as subjects, as social selves, through the ways we are positioned as subjects within discourse. How then, in terms of this investigation, could this placement help to produce individuals with potentially *agentive* outlooks? I will attempt to answer and operationalize this question in the chapters that follow.

Foucauldian and poststructuralist theory is also helpful in noting the "linguistic turn" in social theory and analysis towards understanding the role of discourse in our lives as social beings. This turn, notes Luke, was "from an onus on rationality and cognition to one on language and discourse" (in Gee 1990:viii). As a result of the turn, theorists are now more able to focus on people's daily and subtle interactions through discourse in studying issues of power and domination. I take exception to the extreme poststructuralist notion that we are almost completely positioned and predetermined as social subjects through discourse, and that this process is beyond our conscious control. I agree, however, with its recognition of the *central role* discourse plays in how we are positioned as subjects, and how we come to see and understand ourselves in the world. This notion of the importance of discourse is key in constructing the theoretical framework that informs this study of critical student agency.

Through examining the work of Gramsci, Foucault and the poststructuralists, I have attempted to theoretically trace the notion of agency during this century. While not offering a completely exhaustive theoretical review of the term, my goal was to detail my understanding of agency as it has been influenced by some of the major thinkers for whom the idea has been important—both those who have elaborated and supported the notion, and those who have sought to challenge it. But for the purposes of this study, which examines the kinds of social practices that foster or inhibit the development of agency in one classroom setting, it is important to also review theories in *education* that have specifically dealt with student agency, in particular, critical student agency. The following section, therefore, will seek to elaborate the notion of "student agency" from the perspective of theorists working in the tradition of critical pedagogy, namely, Paulo Freire, Peter McLaren, Kathleen Weiler, Henry Giroux, Antonia Darder, Joe Kincheloe and Michael Apple. This will offer a more contextualized understanding of agency in schools—a "critical" understanding.

Critical Pedagogical Theory: Agency In and Out of Classrooms

Knowledge is relevant only when it begins with the experiences students bring with them from the surrounding culture; it is critical only when these experiences are shown to sometimes be problematic. . .and it is transformative only when students begin to use the knowledge to help empower others, including individuals in the surrounding community.

—**Paulo Freire (1985:189-190)**

The theoretical roots of "critical pedagogy" extend back to the work of Antonio Gramsci on the one hand (as described above), and the "critical theory" of the Frankfurt School on the other. This section begins, therefore, with a brief description of the critical theory of the Frankfurt School.

The Frankfurt School
"Critical social theory" began in the 1920s at the Institute for Social Research—later more commonly known as the "Frankfurt School," under Theodor Adorno (1950, 1973), Max Horkheimer (1940, 1947), and Herbert Marcuse (1964, 1987)—among others (Giroux 1997). While abandoning the determinism of modernist social theory (including structuralist Marxism), and indeed, offering a "blistering critique of the Enlightenment" (Aronowitz

1994:248), these theorists tried to account for and deal with contemporary social issues and problems. In their research and theorizing, they focused on issues such as technological domination, authoritarianism, mass culture, commodification and the role of psychoanalytic theory, from a *neo*-Marxist perspective (Adorno 1973; Best & Kellner 1991; Horkheimer 1947). While presupposing much of Marx's theory of social formations, critical theory attempted to break with the "economistic bias of Marxist social theory" (Aronowitz 1994:117).

Although not able to read and comment on each other's work at the time of its production,[7] the critical theorists of Frankfurt touched on many of the same issues raised earlier by Gramsci, specifically, those that dealt with culture and its relation to economic and other structures (Adorno 1950; Marcuse 1987; Morrow & Torres 1995). Through their early studies of mass communication and authoritarianism—and their experiences in 1930s Germany before moving into exile in the United States—their work came to focus on the role popular culture plays in either challenging or, more often than not, buttressing bourgeois class interests (Adorno 1950).[8] They were interested in understanding how we as human beings slowly begin to accept, and eventually even take part in, our own social and economic domination by others *via* culture—specifically, popular culture—and how this can undermine the socialist project of economic liberation (Agger 1991; Giroux 1983).

Critical social theorists from the Frankfurt School onward have attempted to go beyond modernist/structuralist determinisms and acknowledge both the potential limiting nature of sociocultural formations and individuals' ability to still act agentively within them (Morrow & Torres 1995). While there is certainly a range of thought within critical theory, there is a generally shared belief that the construction and production of individuals' subject positions is a collective social process that occurs discursively from situation to situation between individuals and groups. From this perspective, there are multiple selves and multiple identities (Bauman 1995). Critical theory not only takes exception to the determinisms and structuralism of modernism, but also with radical poststructuralism's diffusion of collective political struggle and agency beyond exclusively local sites. For the theorists at the

Frankfurt School, "Freedom consist[s] in the capacity of actors to make themselves subjects" (Aronowitz 1994:112), thus allowing for acts of individual and collective agency. These and other issues have been taken up within critical *pedagogical* theory by writers such as Freire (1970, 1985), McLaren (1995, 1997), Weiler (1988, 1997), Giroux (1992), Darder (1991), Kincheloe (1990, 1991), Apple (1982), Torres (1994) and Morrow & Torres (1995), among others. Their thoughts converge around the importance of moving beyond totalizing Enlightenment notions of truth and dogmatic adherence to meta-narratives, while at the same time taking seriously the need for individual and collective struggle and action against oppression; that is, agency.

The most influential educational criticalist, worldwide, has been Paulo Freire. In the section below, his work, and how this work contributes to an understanding of critical student agency, will be highlighted.

Freirean Pedagogical Theory: Towards the Development of a Critical Student Agency

> *I refuse to write a how-to manual or provide a step-by-step recipe...When a North American educator reads my work, does not agree with all I say...but feels touched by my writings, rather than merely following me, he or she should begin [their] practice by trying to critically comprehend the contextual conditions of where I worked...Educators must also investigate all of these conditions in their own contexts.*
>
> **—Paulo Freire (Freire & Macedo 1987:134-135)**

Freirean pedagogy has as its goals the liberation of students from oppressive realities they face in their daily lives (Freire 1970, 1985), the development within students of attitudes and capacities to view themselves as capable of taking action on their world in order to change it (Freire 1970; Freire & Macedo 1987, 1998; McLaren 1989, 1997), and the enhancement of student "literacies" and "academic competencies" (Freire 1970; Freire & Macedo 1987; Frankenstein 1992).

Freirean pedagogy seeks to make visible the political nature of schooling, and the effects of unequal, often oppressive, power relations that characterize schooling and the larger late capitalist, post-Fordist society within which we live. Freire's theory of teaching and learning challenges widely held pedagogical truths, with particular emphasis placed on rebuking myths of educational "meritocracy" which attempt to present schooling, and the acquisition of literacy, as individual and neutral processes. Freirean theory seeks to uncover who benefits and who is disenfranchised within educational systems steeped in these so-called "meritocratic" practices (Freire 1985, 1994; McLaren 1986, 1994a).

From a Freirean perspective, people should be seen as "historical subjects" capable of transforming their *own* lived realities as they see them (Aronowitz 1994; Apple 1995:xiii), as "subjects" who act on the world, as opposed to "objects" who are acted upon by others (Freire 1970; Freire & Horton 1990). At the heart of Freire's approach is that learners *re*-form their identities in opposition to perceived societal problems (Freire & Faundez 1992). As Giroux notes:

> [Education] for Freire is inherently a political project in which men and women assert their right and responsibility not only to read, understand, and transform their own experiences, but also to reconstitute their relationships with the larger society. (in Freire & Macedo 1987:7)

That is, students are encouraged to take up subject positions as critical analysts and agents.

Critical teachers following this philosophy are encouraged to engage learners in discussions and investigations of their lived realities and problematic situations. The concerns, needs and personal experiences of the students are at the center of this process. Open-ended cultural and political themes are collectively investigated by the students and teacher in order to generate discussion and to propose actions to solve learners' concerns and problems (McLaren 1989; Shor & Freire 1987; Spener 1990). Through the application of this theory, it is hoped that critical practitioners will facilitate students' development and eventual manifestation of "critical consciousness," what Freire has called "conscientization" (Freire 1970, 1993; McLaren 1994b; Pruyn 1994a). Freire & Rámos define conscientization as, "learning to perceive social, political, and economic contradictions and to take action against the oppressive elements of reality" (Freire 1970:19); that is, the development of a critical student identity toward the world that could then lead to critical student agency.

McNeil (1985), in describing Freire's notion of conscientization, defines it as "the process by which...active learners achieve a deep awareness both of the sociocultural reality that shapes their lives, and of their ability to transform that reality" (37). In developing this critical consciousness, Freire's pedagogy calls for the use of dynamic discursive interactions to develop students' critical understandings within the areas of education, economics, politics and culture (Giroux & McLaren 1992). According to Freire (1970), this critical analytical capacity on the part of the students—the development of critical agentive stances toward the world—is realized as students *engage* the problematic themes of their lives during pedagogic and other encounters. Further, students are encouraged to take collective and individual actions on problematic situations in their lives in order to change them, and then to relate these experiences to classroom learning. In this way, students learn to read the "word" through their reading (and *re*-reading) of their "world" (Freire & Macedo 1987). Through this process, as students become more critically aware of education and language, and their liberatory or repressive potentials, they further increase their ability to be critically conscious (Fariclough 1992b; Janks & Ivanic 1992); to be critical agents.

In summarizing the aims of Freirean pedagogy, Antonia Darder notes that "students discover themselves as historical social subjects with the power to transform their world" (1992:302). According to Freirean theory, classrooms should be places where teachers and students attempt to encounter, and then transform, oppressive power relations based on distinctions such as class, gender, race, language and sexual orientation (Freire & Macedo 1987, 1998; Weiler 1988, 1997; Weiler & Mitchell 1992). At the core, the goal of Freirean pedagogy is not just to assist students in developing various literate and academic competencies, but also to assist students in using these and other skills to develop critical *consciousness* about the social and political conditions of their lives and to take transformative actions—be they small or large (Freire 1970; McLaren 1989, 1997; Shor 1993).

What Freirean pedagogical theory represents is a move toward critical student agency, an agency that is characterized by a critical way of viewing the world (whether it is called "conscientization" or "critical consciousness") and acting on the world—as mediated, *but not determined by*, discourse. We often tacitly accept the way people with power define us, the way they attempt to position us as powerless "objects."[9] To break with this limiting view of self, to take up transformative subject positions, and to then take action based on these new views of self, is to be an agent, a critical agent. A student who assumes such a position is a "critical student agent." This project of assisting students in taking up counter-hegemonic subject positions, within and outside of classrooms, is at the heart of Freirean philosophy.

This is where Freire and Gramsci converge across time. For Gramsci, the working class (along with other strategic groups) takes sociocultural action and begins to form a counter-hegemony that will either change the social order on its own, or will precede and encourage, a revolutionary overthrow of oppressive economic and political forces. For Freire (1970), students ("students/teachers") and teachers ("teachers/students") begin to act as social agents as they are inspired by radical teachers ("cultural workers"[10]) through dialogue and praxis.

From Freirean theory, I will specifically draw on the notions of the development of critical consciousness, evolving views of self and inclination toward action taking, through dialogue and discourse; that is, the development of critical student agency. This study focuses on how, in one setting, critical student agency was fostered or hindered through discourse *via* an examination of students' daily, face-to-face interactions and social practices in the classroom. Such an examination will provide critical pedagogical theorists, researchers and practitioners, who are interested in understanding and advancing their liberatory project, with empirical tools as they seek to understand how critical student agency is developed in actual school settings. In this way, I hope to address a serious gap in the current critical literature.

The work of Paulo Freire, as well as that of Gramsci and the Frankfurt School, has inspired many other thinkers and researchers to pursue and broaden the field of critical pedagogy. The work of several of the most prominent of these critical pedagogical theorists, especially that of Peter McLaren, will be the focus of the following section.

Advancing Agency and Addressing the Postmodern:
McLaren, Weiler, Giroux, Darder, Kincheloe and Apple
Weiler (1988, 1997), Giroux (Giroux 1992; Giroux & McLaren
1992), Darder (1991), Kincheloe (1990), Apple (1993), and especially McLaren (1994c, 1995, 1997), have not only further advanced critical pedagogy, but they have also successfully addressed many of the criticisms leveled against the field by feminist
(Gore 1993; Luke & Gore 1992; O'Hanlon 1988) and poststructuralist (Laclau & Mouffe 1985; Lyotard 1984) theorists, who
posit the existence of multiple sites of power and oppression, and
our participation in our own, and others', subjugation. Through
examining and critiquing some of their major contributions to the
field of critical pedagogy, I hope to add other voices and further
layers of meaning to my central theme in this chapter of critical
student agency.

Peter McLaren.

> [What is needed is a] new socialist imaginary grounded not in specific
> forms of rationality, but in forms of detotalizing agency and the expansion
> of the sphere of radical democracy to new forms of social life.

—Peter McLaren (1995:24)

Peter McLaren, whose work has been influential in North America,
Latin America, Europe, Asia and Africa—it has been translated
into at least five different languages—is both a leading intellectual
in the field of critical pedagogy and also one of the top Marxist
theorists working in the social sciences today. He has also had
much to contribute in debates in the areas of student agency,
poststructuralism and discourse. According to McLaren's critical
pedagogical theory (1989, 1995, 1997), our current postmodern
condition, and the role that discourse may play in *partially* prede-
termining our subject positions, does not rule out our potential as
active historical social subjects, as agents, capable of changing the
world. While recognizing the "predatory culture" of the postmodern times within which we are living, McLaren notes the important
contributions of poststructuralist theory. He also cautions (1995),
however, that "we should not forfeit the opportunity of theorizing

both teachers and students as historical agents of resistance" (223), as poststructuralist theory might have us do.

McLaren, like others working in critical pedagogy, draws on the work of Gramsci and the Frankfurt School, and also carefully incorporates neo-Lyotardian poststructuralist perspectives (1995) into his work, while continually advocating student agency. Synthesizing the work of these poststructural theorists, and the pedagogical theory of Paulo Freire, McLaren calls for the development within students of subject positions as critical social agents, which he defines (1995:15) as "knowing how to live contingently and provisionally without the certainty of knowing the truth, yet at the same time, with the courage to take a stand on issues of human suffering, domination, and oppression."

In his recent work (McLaren 1997; McLaren & Fischman, In Press; McLaren, Fischman, Serra & Antelo 1998), McLaren has called for a return to a Marxist- and neo-Gramscian-inspired focus and *re*-emphasis on issues of working class domination and oppression by bourgeois sectors—especially in this current climate of growing, diversifying and strengthening global capitalist/corporate power and control. If we lose sight of the central role class relations and exploitation play, in educational contexts and elsewhere, he cautions, our analyses will be incomplete and our successes in struggling for social justice few and far between.

The struggle for agency and social justice, notes McLaren (1995), in not an easy one:

> Agency is never complete, as subjects are continually being produced within and by relations of power and systematic structures of exclusion, disempowerment, abjection, deauthorization and erasure. (236)

Kathleen Weiler.

Kathleen Weiler (1988, 1991, 1997), as a critical feminist, has argued both against non-critical feminist pedagogical approaches which hold that a dismantling of patriarchy (alone) is what is needed to empower and liberate students and the larger society, and social reproductionist approaches in education which claim that schools are autonomous sites of social reproduction where students are "educated" to fill specific slots in our unjust capitalist society based on class, gender and racial differences.

To the former group (non-critical feminist pedagogical theorists) she responds that while patriarchy is indeed a disabling and oppressive ideology and manifestation, its elimination will not automatically erase other forms of oppression based on social class, race, language, *et cetera*. In response to the liberal wing within feminist pedagogy—which has as its main goal the reform of texts, practices and policies in education against gender bias— she notes that it is important to recognize the key role played by capitalist economic structures and forms of domination. She suggests a strategy for liberation that includes not just collective opposition to patriarchy, racism and homophobia, but also, crucially, opposition to capital and its negative effects (1998).

To the latter group (social reproductionist theorists) she responds that their theoretically totalizing approach to understanding the role of actual students and teachers within the educational system rules out the possibility for "resistance" and "human agency," which she believes are key if we are serious in the struggle for social justice. Instead, she encourages (1988) a critical pedagogy that

> will recognize both human agency and the production of knowledge and culture and will at the same time take into account the power of material and ideological structures. This dialectic between individual consciousness and structural determinants has led...[critical pedagogical theorists] to seek more developed theories of ideology, hegemony, and resistance... (13)

Henry Giroux.

Henry Giroux's critical pedagogy has been influenced by Lukacs, Gramsci, the Frankfurt School, Aronowitz, Giddens, the early writings of Marx and various *neo*-Marxist theorists (Giroux 1994), and has been critical of the over-deterministic views of structuralist Marxism. Giroux takes up Gramsci's call for counter-hegemony, and theorizes teachers as "transformative intellectuals" and "cultural workers" who should foster critical analytical capacities and agency among students (1992). While working within the Frankfurt tradition, Giroux is careful not to be pulled into the pessimism evident in much of Adorno's work (1950). Giroux maintains an utopian social vision and encourages the use of a "language of possibility" both in pedagogical theory and practice (1984, 1992). Giroux is also influenced by poststructuralist and postmodernist themes whereby the working class is no longer at the center of *all* agentive activity. According to Giroux, there are multiple forms of oppression *and* multiple potential critical agents who can take stands against that oppression (Giroux & McLaren 1992). These agents include groups such as women, people of color, children, queers (lesbian, gay, bisexual and transgender people) and workers. Like Apple, he carefully notes the *potential* poststructuralist theories represent for a "flight from politics" (1988:61). Both Giroux and Apple advocate a "radical democratic populism" that seems to have "socialist implications" without openly referring to socialism or socialist projects directly (Morrow & Torres 1995:330 & 335). Indeed, perhaps noting a move away from *neo*-Marxist politics, Giroux uses the term "resistance" in place of "revolution" (Morrow & Torres 1995:330).

Antonia Darder.

Developing a critical pedagogy for bicultural students—a critical bicultural theoretical and pedagogical vision—has been at the center of the work of Antonia Darder (1991, 1995a, 1995b). More specifically, her work has focused on: (1) creative and critical ways we can make our classrooms and other educational settings more emancipatory—through more empowering classroom structures, materials, forms of active student research & participation, and understanding the dynamics of culture and power (1991); and, (2) successful forms of liberatory practice being used with students of color and working class students today (1995a, 1995b). Most pertinent to this study have been her writings on issues of resistance and counter-hegemony as encouraged by certain critical teachers with the aforementioned groups of students. She notes (1991) that:

> Critical educators adhere to the philosophical principle that all people have the capacity to make meaning of their lives and to resist oppression. But they also recognize the fact that the capacity to resist and understand is limited and influenced by issues of class, race, and gender. People will use whatever means at hand or whatever power they can employ to meet their needs and assert their humanity. But, unfortunately, since the solutions they often select arise from the ascribed beliefs and values of

the dominant society, they may in fact lead themselves and others deeper into forms of domination and oppression. (88-89)

Joe Kincheloe.

Joe Kincheloe's examinations of history and historians (1990, 1991), social studies and the social sciences (1985, 1988), and teacher education as it currently exists and as it *could* exist (1989, 1993), have led to unique analyses of ideology, agency and social change from a criticalist perspective. For this study, his work on agency (1990, 1991) has been particularly instructive. In elaborating on the negative effects of closeted and implicit teacher ideology[11] on student agency, he notes (1990):

> It constricts human agency by legitimating systems of domination, by concealing the means by which domination is effected, and by defying transitory historical moments, i.e., presenting "what is" as if it was natural and just, and could have been no other way. (32).

On the other hand, outed and explicit teacher ideology

> enables human action by constructing concepts, categories, and ideas through which individuals come to understand their sociopolitical context and as a result of such understanding are empowered to change for the better. (1990:32)

In other words, at the very least, teachers need to be honest and open about, and self-critical of, their ideologies and pedagogical philosophies for the potential of critical student agency to exist.

Michael Apple.

In his early work (*Ideology and Curriculum*, 1979), Michael Apple was strongly influenced by a structuralist Marxist interpretation (see Althusser 1969, 1990) of Gramsci as translated into education by social reproductionists such as Bowles & Gintis (1976). While recognizing the existence of student resistance and agency, Apple originally saw the social order as being largely determined by, and serving, the larger economic functions of society—that is, schools exist to unevenly distribute cultural capital to students, and to sort them into predetermined slots in our capitalist system (Apple 1979). With the publication of *Education and Power* (1982), Apple becomes more critical of this position, and what he now interprets as its overly simplistic views on the relation of cultural practices and economic formations (Apple 1986; Morrow & Torres 1995). This change is partly influenced by Stuart Hall's "cultural studies" (1981, 1986, 1992), the work of neo-Marxist Erik Olin Wright (Wright 1978; Wright, Levine & Sober 1992), and Paul Willis' ethnography on student resistance (1977). These theorists and researchers had been exploring the role that culture plays in supporting and/or subverting the capitalist order. With his growing sympathies toward this "cultural Marxism," Apple begins to move closer in his analyses to the work of the Frankfurt School and Gramsci, and becomes more open to poststructuralist and postmodernist orientations. Yet he is cautious in his use of poststructuralism because of its focus on potentially endless multiple centers of power. Apple notes, "We can multiply forms of domination to such an extent that there are no meaningful organizations left to combat oppression" (1993:176).

The Freirean/Critical Approach Taken in this Study

According to critical pedagogical theorists—from Freire (1970, 1993) through McLaren (McLaren 1986, 1995; McLaren & Fischman, In Press)—schools, as a cultural tool of dominant groups, can serve to either entrench the existing hegemonic order, or can be sites of counter-hegemonic activity by "transformative/organic" intellectuals (Giroux 1992; Gramsci 1971). The task of these radical and transformative teacher intellectuals is to strike blows at the dominant hegemony in schools and in society.

Under hegemonic pedagogy, the teacher is the authority who transmits content to students. Teachers are seen as "second mothers or fathers," as bringers of the "word," givers of knowledge, and as providers of intellectual "nutrition" to the hungry and undernourished minds of students (Fischman 1994, 1998; Freire 1985; Pruyn & Fischman 1998). Following this prevalent approach, students are to absorb information/knowledge/facts as delivered to them by the teacher and through official texts. Students are to learn by following the mandates and instructions of the teacher.

From the perspective of hegemonic pedagogy, the focus is on memorization and rote skills—sometimes referred to by its opponents as the "drill, skill and kill" approach. Instructional content, beyond basic "skills," is seen as a finite set of "classic" works and facts, and is often associated with the Western (Western European/North American) cultural canon. This mode of educational practice is referred to by Freire (1970) as "banking education." Under banking education, students are seen as empty vessels who need to be filled up with knowledge and "truth" by the teacher. Educational thinkers and policy makers such as Hirsch (1987), Ravitch (1990, 1991) and Bennett (1992), as well as educational movements such as "back-to-basics," have been associated with this approach to teaching and learning. I will refer to this set of classroom relationships and modes of teacher-student interaction as "hegemonic pedagogical practices"; that is, educational practices that reinforce, rather than challenge, the dominant cultural, political, economic and educational order.

It is the goal of Freirean pedagogy to create a counter-logic, a world view and a mode of operating, in both classrooms and the world, that seeks to transform this dominant way of interacting in classrooms. And indeed, it was just this type of Freirean orientation that ostensibly drove the work at the community-based education project that is the focus of this study.

The following section will review and critique the literature on Freirean/critical *practice*. An emphasis will be placed on research that has been similar to my own in order to demonstrate how this present study makes a unique theoretical and practical contribution to the field of critical pedagogy.

Freirean Pedagogical Practice:
Striving for Agency, Creating Change

The Paulo Freire of today has a certain coherence with the Paulo Freire of yesterday. The Paulo Freire of yesterday has not died. I mean to say that I have been living during all these years...But the Paulo Freire of today necessarily brings with him the marks of experience. For example, the Paulo Freire of today had the opportunity, had the luck, to know Nicaragua. In my 60 years I did not know Nicaragua, not the dominated Nicaragua. The Paulo Freire of today had the luck to live the experience of Chile, Allende's transitional Chile, the frustrated coup d'etat Chile. The Paulo Freire of today had the opportunity to know Tanzania, to participate in the profound transformations because of the expulsion of the colonizers in Angola, Guinea-Bissao, Cabo Verde and Sao Tomé...Therefore, it would be a disaster, it

would be very sad, if I hadn't learned with these five or six historical mo-
ments, if today I were to continue doing the same thing which brought me to
exile twenty years ago, first in Bolivia and then in Chile.

—**Paulo Freire (in Torrez 1986:31-32)**

Unfortunately, the educational literature on research that has examined the development of critical student agency in
Freirean/critical educational settings is not a rich one. It is, however, growing. While there do exist a number of studies that have
reported on the *general* successes or failures of Freirean-oriented
projects, broadly defined, little has been written, on how these
critical learning communities created themselves in the moment-to-
moment practices of classroom life. Even fewer studies elaborate
how liberatory practices lead to specific transformative action—or
lack thereof—on the part of students. Understanding what these
studies have found, albeit with foci that are different than the one
in this study, will prove useful nonetheless in situating this research project in the larger practical critical pedagogical literature.
Following, then, is a sampling of some of these studies, and a critique based on my particular focus on the development of student
agency within discourse.

Over the past thirty years there have been many attempts to
put into practice the ideas of Paulo Freire and those theorists
working in the tradition he inspired. Freire worked directly with
many governments and non governmental groups around the
world, over the last several decades, in helping to plan and carry
out adult literacy programs with the goal of developing students'
academic competence and critical awareness. These groups include the governments of Tanzania, Allende's Chile, Guinea-
Bissau, Sandinista Nicaragua, Sao Tomé, Príncipe, Brazil, revolutionary Granada, Angola's MPLA—and later the government of
Angola—Mozambique's FRELIMO and Cabo Verde. Freire's
writings and ideas have also inspired, although without his direct
participation, critical literacy projects in Cuba, China, Honduras,
Puerto Rico and in El Salvador *via* the FMLN (*El Frente Farabundo
Martí para la Liberación Nacional*/The Farabundo Martí Front for
National Liberation) (Arnove 1981; Bandera 1981; Freire 1970;
Freire & Macedo 1987; Pruyn 1992; Torrez 1986; Vázquez-

MARc PRuYN

Camarena 1987). And many of these attempts at Freirean-oriented practice have been well documented.

Probably the most dramatic and successful attempt at Freirean practice took place in revolutionary Nicaragua in 1980, after the leftist FSLN (*El Frente Sandinista para la Liberación Nacional*/The Sandinista Front for National Liberation) organized and carried out the unprecedented "Nicaraguan National Literacy Crusade" only months after having led a popular uprising against the U.S.-backed Somoza dictatorship. As part of the Crusade, tens of thousands of literate Nicaraguan youth from the urban centers were trained in the Freirean approach and sent out to all parts of the country to teach their compatriots to read and write and also to develop within them revolutionary and critical analytical attitudes (Chacón & Pozas 1980; Hirshon & Butler 1983; Pruyn 1992; Vázquez-Camarena 1987). Under this national mobilization, Nicaragua's illiteracy rate dropped from over 50% to well under 25% in less than a year—some claim it went as low as 12% (Arnove 1981; Arnove & Dewees 1991).

A second result of the Crusade was that hundreds of thousands of average Nicaraguans, many of the students and teachers involved in the project, became politically active for first time in their lives in the country's many popular organizations and movements, and in the government itself, where they had more control over problematic issues in their lives. In essence, as illiteracy rates decreased, levels of critical student agency increased. In the middle of the Literacy Crusade, the United States organized and began to fund a large-scale counter-revolutionary war against the Nicaraguan government and people in the guise of the *Contras*—a band of mostly former Somoza National Guardsmen (with infamous human rights' records) that targeted the civilian population, especially those connected with social services sectors, such as teachers.

As the Nicaraguan government was compelled to direct more financial and human resources toward the defense of the country, little was left for literacy maintenance programs, or for education generally, and illiteracy rates began to climb again (Arnove 1981; Arnove & Dewees 1991; Chacón & Pozas 1980; Hirshon & Butler 1983; Karliner & Faber 1986; Lappé & Medea 1986; Pruyn 1992; Puiggrós 1983, 1986; Torres 1990, 1991; Vázquez-Camarena

1987). While helpful in showing, in broad terms, how the attempt at Freirean practice was successful in Nicaragua (if only for a short time, due to North American aggression), the accounts and reports describing the Crusade do not show what it was in classrooms, in interactions between students and teachers, that made it a success; that drove down illiteracy, and drove up student agency.

Another example of Freirean practice on a grand scale is the case of revolutionary Grenada under Maurice Bishop and the "New Jewel Movement." Their literacy campaign, begun after Grenada's 1979 leftist revolution, reduced illiteracy levels in the small country and helped to develop the participants' views of self as active participants in the new revolutionary society through participation in the Grenada's popular political and social movements and new governmental structures. In this case as well, illiteracy rates were shown to decrease—although not as dramatically as in Nicaragua—and levels of student agency (which I am associating here with cultural, civic and political participation in formal and non-formal institutions alike) were shown to increase (La Belle 1986; Torres 1990, 1991). This progress was halted, and the gains rolled back, after the 1983 CIA-linked assassination of Bishop, and the subsequent U.S. military invasion of the small island nation (Chadwick & Albrecht 1989; Gilmore 1984; Hickling-Hudson 1988; Jules 1993; Pruyn 1992). The reports and studies of the educational events in revolutionary Grenada are supportive of the claims made by critical pedagogical theorists, that through empowering students as critical change agents, hegemonic structures can be re-envisioned and re-created along the lines of a more just society. However, these studies are less than specific as to the classroom or discursive interactions that may have been responsible for these positive changes.

One can also find examples of Freirean-oriented practice in the United States. A very prominent example of a project that links literacy development and social empowerment to the development of critical consciousness and action is that of the Highlander Folk School. Highlander was formed, and functioned for many years, before Freire began his theoretical writings, and therefore was not directly influenced by Freire's theories or practice. The practice of the Folk School, however, was very similar to that advocated by

Freire. The example of Highlander shows how a very similar pedagogical and theoretical approach could be independently arrived at, and how this approach of transformative teaching and learning could be successful. Myles Horton formed Highlander in the working class Appalachian Mountains of the United States in the 1930s. A radical Christian teacher, Horton's inspiration came from George S. Counts' social reconstructionism, Reinhold Neibur's radical view of Christianity, Denmark's Folk School movement and from the writings of Marx (Adams 1972, 1975).

Highlander helped to educate, make literate and politically empower, many groups of people, including large numbers of trade unionists and potential unionists from the region, many regular "country folk," and thousands of African Americans. The Highlander project was implemented through the use of a curriculum and a philosophy that focused on understanding and changing students' real life problems—closely foreshadowing Freire's pedagogy that would find voice in Brazil of the 1960s. It has been argued that the African Americans who gained literacy at Highlander, and therefore the right to vote under the Jim Crow laws in the segregated South of the United States of the 1940s and 1950s, played a pivotal role in the civil rights movement that was soon to follow (Adams 1972). At Highlander, many people gained literacy, academic skills and became sociopolitically active for the first time in their lives, becoming change agents in very real ways that directly effected them: as union organizers and militants, as local social workers and as agitators for basic civil and human rights in the region for all people (Adams 1972, 1975). While showing how a transformative/political educational project similar to that elaborated by Freire was possible in a North American setting, the accounts of Adams (1972, 1975) suffer from the same lack of classroom/interpersonal specificity as do the reports on the Nicaraguan and Grenadan experiences. The studies of Highlander elaborate how graduates from their programs manifested critical student agency in taking political, cultural and social action, but they do not indicate *how* this student critical agency was developed within the classroom.

Besides these and other large-scale successful attempts to put Freire's theories into practice, there have been other small-scale attempts. For example, in a study of an English instruction high school in pre-democratic Botswana, South Africa, McKenzie (1992) found that through a Freirean-inspired critical language teaching program, students were able to focus on critical analyses of the school's discursive practices and come to see how meaning could be "deconstructed" and then "reconstructed" to empower students through their use of language. Solorzano (1989) conducted a study of the application of the Freirean approach in a community college classroom in the United States and found that one group of students was able to successfully develop critical views of self and analytic capacities. Not only did the learners develop new identities as empowered social subjects through following the Freirean approach, but they also took concrete action as agents as they solidified these identities. This group of students was successfully able to implement a boycott against films which negatively portrayed Chicanos/as (Solorzano 1989).

Each of these applications and studies of practice appear to demonstrate that by following the philosophy and general method of empowerment and action advanced by Freire, McLaren and other critical pedagogical theorists, students can come to see themselves as critical analysts and actors. These studies, though, do not tell us how these critical agentive views of self were *created*. While important and helpful theoretically and politically, they are too general. They largely stop at the level of description. The Nicaraguan, Grenadan and Highlander[12] examples all fall into this category. These attempts at Freirean practice were successful (Adams 1975; Arnove 1981; La Belle 1986). The studies analyzing this practice show how they were carried out generally and what some of the larger measurable outcomes were—such as levels of literacy achieved and amount of increased political participation. However, these studies do not provide us with an understanding of what specifically occurred in classrooms between the teachers and the students that *made* these attempts at Freirean practice successful. The smaller-scale studies do bring us closer to the classrooms where Freirean practice was being attempted. They too, however, tend to stop at the level of description of what general classroom practices brought about critical growth and not the teacher-student and student-student discursive specifics of *how* students came to see themselves critical agents.

Many studies have looked at Freirean/critical pedagogy, but few have done so with data from classrooms. Additionally, none that I was able to find have tried to explicate why, through regularized and on-going discursive interactions, various attempts at Freirean practice have either been successful or unsuccessful in achieving their goals. This study examines an attempted instantiation of Freirean practice by looking at data from one specific classroom, and in so doing, will seek to understand and unpackage the types of social and discursive practices that fostered or hindered the development of critical student agency among the students involved. By taking such an approach, this study will fill a void in the literature on Freirean pedagogical practice that, to date, has not looked at classroom discourse data to understand the process of social formation of students as potential critical social agents.

Focusing on discourse as an analytical technique in understanding the social practices of classrooms, and the impact of these practices on student academic and social development, has been successfully employed in numerous studies (Ivanic & Simpson 1992; Gee 1990; Gutierrez 1991c, 1992, 1994; Gutierrez & Larson 1994; Gutierrez, Rymes & Larson 1995; Pruyn 1994a; Pruyn & Fischman 1998). Focusing on discourse can provide researchers with a means for discerning how certain social practices come into being, are maintained or change over time. It would serve this study well, therefore, to provide a more detailed elaboration of the term "discourse" and how it is used in this work. The following section will focus on how researchers have used discourse analysis to understand social practices and processes within classrooms, and how I use "critical discourse analysis" in identifying the development of critical student agency in this study.

A Focus on Discourse: Searching for Agency in Everyday Practices and Talk

The common understanding of the word "discourse" is the written and oral language we use with one another as human beings. But there is also a broader understanding of what constitutes "discourse." This more encompassing definition includes our ways of speaking and writing, but also our ways of behaving, thinking, valuing, interacting and feeling. James Paul Gee (1990) describes "Discourses" (capital "D") as being systems of "sayings-doings-thinkings-feelings-valuings." We are all members of several discourse communities at the same time, and "each Discourse represents one of our ever multiple identities" (Gee 1990:xix).

But why analyze discourse? If our identities as potential social agents are formed through the subject positions we take up and are placed in through discourse, then we must specifically analyze discursive practices between people in order to comprehend how these understandings of self are constructed over time.

Researchers Ochs (1993), from applied linguistics, and Gutierrez, Stone and Larson (In Press), from education, elaborate a *sociocultural* understanding of identity and discourse in which identity formation occurs between individuals in social interaction through discourse. Ochs (1993) notes the connection between language and identity, positing that, "speakers attempt to establish the social identities of themselves and others through verbally performing certain social acts and displaying certain stances" (288).[13] From this point of view, identities are "manifold, shifting, momentary...multiple...blended...[and] even blurred..." (298). This notion of the construction of social identities through discourse is a key concept in this study. Specifically, there is a focus on students' formation of critical agentive identities through the discursive stances they assume, or accept, as they interact with their teachers and classmates.

In examining educational contexts, Gutierrez, Stone & Larson (In Press) echo a sociocultural position on identity. In their study of "narrative" in an elementary classroom, they state that, "It is in...[the] unfolding of the social practices of the classroom that...[we] can observe how the formation of identity is discursively constructed" (31). For these researchers, identity is "mediated through social interaction" (Gutierrez, Stone & Larson, In Press:17). The "construction of identity...is best understood in what people do in joint participation with one another" (Gutierrez, Rymes & Larson 1995:2). Students and teachers naturally develop identities, and take up subject positions, as they participate in learning activities in the social world (Lave & Wenger 1991:36). According to Gutierrez, Rymes & Larson (1995), relations of power *between* people shape the identities *of* those people through their on-going and regular discursive and linguistic interactions. These sociocultural theorists not only hold that identities are formed in social interactions with others, but that these interactions are intimately tied with power relations between individuals and groups. Put another way, power relations, discourse and social identities are mutually informing.

Weiler (1988) further elaborates the role discourse plays, as understood from a criticalist perspective, in classrooms:

> Classroom discourse reveals meaning mutually created by teachers and students. It is never neutral, but is always situated in the context of a socially and historically defined present. Teachers and students use language to assert their own power and to try to create sense for themselves out of a complex social setting. (128-129)

"Critical" discourse theorist Norman Fairclough (1992a) has noted that "discourse as a political practice establishes, sustains and changes power relations, and the collective entities...between which power relations obtain" (67). Building on Foucauldian and Gramscian notions of power, Fairclough asserts that these power relations, far from being overt and outwardly coercive—although this *can* be the case—are more often than not "invisible." Further, those individuals who produce and/or suffer under various oppressive relations of power are not always aware of the existence of these relations, for they tend to become "regularized" in ongoing social practices (Fariclough 1992b:3 & 6).

As Fairclough notes, "ideologies embedded in discursive practices are most effective when they become naturalized and achieve a status of 'common sense'" (1992a:87). This extends Gramsci's understanding of "common sense" and Foucault and Freire's notions of power and social control. Foucault (1977a) holds that modern power is not (always) imposed from above, but rather, is often developed from below in "microtechniques" within institutions (143). Further, as one participates in various institutions and settings, power relations are learned and become central to an individual's identity (Foucault 1977a). Gramsci, writing earlier in the century, developed a similar notion of power and control when he noted that hegemonic power can change over time, can be contested and is maintained partially through consent (1971). For these theorists and researchers, doing analyses of discourse is key to understanding the social processes from which they emanate, and with which they are closely tied.

In his volume *Discourse and Social Change* (1992a), Fairclough distinguishes between critical and non-critical approaches to discourse analysis. Within non-critical discourse analysis, he includes the work of Sinclair & Coulthard (1975), Sacks & Schegloff,[14] Labov & Fanshel (1977), and Potter & Wetherell (1987). While praising the significant theoretical and practical tools and techniques these theorists have brought to the field of discourse analysis, Fairclough is also critical of them. Fairclough claims, for example, that non-critical discourse analysis does not make the connections between people's micro-discursive interactions and discourse's larger role in maintaining existing oppressive macro power relations between individuals, and individuals and institutions,[15] or its potential liberatory nature.[16] Put another way, non-critical discourse analysis does not relate power relations that are present in discursive interaction to larger social phenomena and does not facilitate the asking of questions such as: How does discourse contribute to counter-hegemonic social action or transformation? How does it reconstitute or maintain power relations and existing hegemony?

Luke comments:

> [M]any sociolinguistic and linguistic analyses of texts pay close attention to patterns of language in use but stop short of explicating how discourses evidenced in local contexts have political and ideological consequences. (1995:11)

This study uses some of the analytical tools and techniques offered by non-critical discourse analysts and researchers. However, with the political nature of schooling central to the Freirean pedagogy and theory that drives both this study and the adult literacy project that is its object, it is necessary to employ a version of discourse analysis that is theoretically and sociopolitically more encompassing. Luke (1995) describes a *critical* discourse analysis that could serve just this function:

> Critical discourse analysis sets out to generate agency among students, teachers, and others by giving them tools to see how texts represent the social and natural world...[It] begins from a poststructuralist skepticism toward the assumption that people have singular, essential social iden-

tities or fixed cultural, social class, or gendered characteristics. It assumes that subjectivities are strategically constructed and contested though textual practices and that they are crafted in dynamics of everyday life. (12 & 14)

This approach of *critical* discourse analysis, while employing many of the same analytical methods as the non-criticalists, focuses on the very issues raised by Fairclough and Luke: that discourse, power relations and politics are intimately linked. Fairclough (1992a, 1992b), his colleagues (Ivanic & Simpson 1992; Janks & Ivanic 1992), and other theorists and researchers[17] have called for, and have analytically implemented, a critical discourse analysis that brings together (non-critical) linguistically-oriented discourse analysis and political discourse theory (like the work of Foucault) to systematically study social change (Fariclough 1992a, 1992b). The work of these researchers builds on Foucauldian social analyses in that it deals with instances of actual discursive practice (where Foucault's work does *not* necessarily), and all that is associated with them, and the tools and methods of non-critical discourse analysis. Under Fairclough's approach, discourse is analyzed on three levels: "text description, interaction interpretation, and social action explanation" (1992a:70-91; 1992b:9-12). These levels of discursive analysis are important to Fairclough in that he is building on the work of Foucault (1973, 1977a, 1977b, 1980), and to a lesser extent, the work of Gramsci (1971). Fairclough understands the role language plays, or can play, in the production and maintenance of newer forms of often seemingly "non-coercive" cultural power relations (1992b).

Through critical discourse analysis, it can be seen how particular discursive situations help to form agentive subjectivities that can potentially empower learners. I share Fairclough, Gee, Luke, Gramsci and Foucault's understandings on the power and potential liberatory or coercive nature of language and language use. And, as Gutierrez, Rymes & Larson have noted in examining classrooms from a similar perspective (1995), one can detangle the notions of power construction and identity formation by examining the everyday discursive practices of those classrooms. My goal in Chapters 3 through 6, below, as I begin to deconstruct the forms of social practice at work in the adult literacy classroom whose objective it was to develop students as critical agents, will be to use critical discourse analysis to understand how students' identities—their subject positions—as social agents were produced in daily discursive interaction with their classmates and teachers. Before this, however, I will first describe the methodology I employed in conducting the research and analysis presented in this study.

Notes

1. Linked with and interwoven throughout this discussion on agency shall be an elaboration of the concepts of "hegemony," "counter-hegemony" and "resistance," for these notions are integral to the way this study will consider agency and its manifestation.

2. A "meta-narrative," as I define and use it here, is an all-encompassing philosophical/scientific explanation for social phenomena. In the social sciences, for example, Enlightenment meta-narratives include "capitalism" and "communism."

3. Such as capitalism, patriarchy, racism, homophobia, *et cetera*.

4. Discourse is defined by Foucault as anything written, said or communicated (1972). Luke (1995), in elaborating on the Foucauldian understanding of the nature and function of discourse notes, "Discourse actually defines, constructs and positions human subjects...but [not through]...simple top-down ideological manipulation. Communities participate in discourse in local, often idiosyncratic ways, both resisting and becoming complicit in their own moral regulation. When and where these discourses are internalized by the subject as her or his own constitute the moment of noncoercive discipline *par excellence*" (8-9).

5. See McLaren & Giroux's "Writing from the Margins: Geographies of Identity, Pedagogy, and Power" in McLaren's (1997) *Revolutionary Multiculturalism: Pedagogies of Dissent for the New Millennium.*

6. Others heartily disagree. Mayo (1994), for example, notes that Gramsci's theorizing marked a "decisive break with the official Marxism of the time" (127). For more on this, also see McLaren, Fischman, Serra & Antelo (1998).

7. Gramsci was allowed only limited access to outside reading materials during his incarceration from 1926 until his death in 1937 in Mussolini's prisons. And his notebooks, written in Italian, were not fully compiled or translated into other languages until much later.

8. Gramsci, on the other hand, had more faith in popular culture. Coming from a humble peasant background, and steeped in mass/popular culture, Gramsci believed that members of the working class could rise up as organic intellectuals and inspire their class com-

rades through a re-envisioned, pro-working class interpretation of popular culture—of hegemony—revolutionarily defined (1971). The work of the Frankfurt critical theorists on culture—along with that of Gramsci—would go on to inspire later thinkers in critical pedagogical theory such as Freire, McLaren, Weiler, Giroux, Darder, Kincheloe and Apple, and their work on resistance and agency—which figure prominently in my discussion of the formation of students as critical social agents, below.

9. Individuals and groups who occupy positions of power often attempt to position those who do not as "objects." From my theoretical and philosophical standpoint, however—and from Freire's (1985)—people *cannot be* objects. They can only be either active or passive "social subjects." Yet this does not prevent those who wield power from attempting to position others as objects.

10. What Gramsci calls "organic intellectuals" (1971) and Giroux & McLaren (1992) call "transformative intellectuals."

11. See, also, Gee (1990).

12. I include the Highlander case here as an "attempted Freirean application" because of its striking philosophical and methodological similarities to Freirean theory and practice, not because Horton was directly influenced by Freire's writings and work (which he was not, except toward the end of his life).

13. Behavioral *acts* like "requesting, contradicting or interrupting" and attitudinal *stances* such as "certainty or uncertainty, or as expressing a particular emotional state" (Ochs 1993:288).

14. See Sacks (1972); Sacks, Jefferson & Schegloff (1977); and Sacks, Schegloff & Jefferson (1974).

15. For examples of theory and research that *does* make this connection, see the work of Fairclough 1992a, 1992b; Foucault 1973, 1977a; and Gutierrez, Rymes & Larson 1995.

16. For examples of theory and research that take analyses to *this* level, see the work of Ivanic & Simpson 1992; Fairclough 1992a; Freire 1970; McLaren 1986, 1989; Freire & Macedo 1987, 1998; and Gutierrez, Rymes & Larson 1995.

17. See, for example, the work of "critical linguists" Kress (1988, 1989) and Kress & Hodge (1979), who combine textual analysis, a social theory of language, politics and ideology; the "systemic linguistics" work of Halliday (1978); and the work of Pêcheux (1982), who focuses on the social theory of discourse and political text analysis (Fairclough 1992a).

References

Adams, F. 1972. "Highlander Folk School: 'Getting Information, Going Back, and Teaching It." *Harvard Educational Review* 42: 497-520.

_____. 1975. *Unearthing Seeds of Fire*. Winston-Salem: John F. Blair.

Adorno, T., et al. 1950. *The Authoritarian Personality*. New York: Norton.

_____. 1973 [1966]. *Negative Dialectics*. New York: Seabury.

Agger, B. 1991. *A Critical Theory of Public Life: Knowledge, Discourse and Politics in an Age of Decline*. London: Falmer.

Althusser, L. 1969. *For Marx*. Brewster, B. (Trans.). London: Penguin.

_____. 1990. *Philosophy and the Spontaneous Philosophy of the Scientists: And Other Essays*. Elliot, G., ed. London: Verso.

Apple, M. 1979. *Ideology and Curriculum*. New York: Routledge.

_____. 1982. *Education and Power*. London: Routledge.

_____. 1986. *Teachers and Texts: A Political Economy of Class and Gender Relations in Education*. New York: Routledge.

_____. 1993. *Official Knowledge: Democratic Education in a Conservative Age*. New York: Routledge.

_____. ed., 1995. *Review of Research in Education* 21. Washington, D.C.: American Educational Research Association.

Arnove, R. June, 1981. "The Nicaraguan Literacy Crusade of 1980." *Phi Delta Kappan*, 702-708.

Arnove, R. and Dewees, A. 1991. "Education and Revolution in Nicaragua, 1979-1990." *Comparative Education Review* 35: 92-109.

Aronowitz, S. 1994. *Dead Artists, Live Theories, and Other Cultural Problems*. New York: Routledge.

Bandera, A. 1981. *Paulo Freire: Un Pedagogo*. Bogota: Centro de Estudios para el Desarrollo e Integración de América Latina.

Bauman, Z. 1988. "Is There a Postmodern Sociology?" *Theory, Culture, and Society* 5: 217-237.

_____. 1995. *Life in Fragments: Essays in Postmodern Morality*. Oxford: Blackwell.

Bennett, W. J. 1992. *The De-valuing of America: The Fight for Our Culture and Children*. New York: Summit Books.

Best, S. and Kellner, D. 1991. *Postmodern Theory: Critical Interrogations*. New York: Guilford.

Bowles, S. and Gintis, H. 1976. *Schooling in Capitalist America: Educational Reform and the Contradictions of Economic Life*. New York: Basic Books.

Casey, K. 1993. *I Answer with My Life: Life Histories of Women Teachers Working for Social Change*. New York: Routledge.

Chacón, A. and Pozas, V. 1980. *Cruzada Nacional de Alfabetización*. Managua: Ministerio de Educación.

Chadwick, B. Albrecht, S. 1989. "Educational and Career Aspirations of Secondary School Students in Grenada Following the American Intervention." *Adolescence* 24: 523-540.

Darder, A. 1991. *Culture and Power in the Classroom: A Critical Foundation for Bicultural Education*. Westport: Bergin & Garvey.

_____. 1992. "Book Review of *Pedagogy of the Oppressed*." *The Nation* 255: 301.

_____. 1995a, ed. *Culture and Difference: Critical Perspectives on the Bicultural Experience in the United States*. Westport: Bergin & Garvey.

_____. 1995b, ed. *Bicultural Studies in Education: Transgressive Discourses of Resistance and Possibility*. Claremont: Institute for Education in Transformation.

Derrida, J. 1973. *Speech and Phenomena, and Other Essays on Husserl's Theory of Signs*. Evanston: Northwest University Press.

_____. 1981. *Positions*. Chicago: University of Chicago Press.

_____. 1994. *Specters of Marx: The State of the Debt, the Work of Mourning, & the New International*. London: Routledge.

Fairclough, N. 1992a. *Discourse and Social Change*. Cambridge: Polity.

_____. 1992b, ed. *Critical Language Awareness*. New York: Longman.

Fischman, G. 1994. "Schooling in Argentina in the 1990s: Is There Any Room Left for Popular Education and Critical Pedagogy? Paper presented at the 1994 Meeting of the Comparative and International Education Society. San Diego, California.

_____. 1998. "Donkeys and Superteachers: Structural Adjustment and Popular Education in Latin America." *International Review of Education* 42: 177-199.

Foucault, M. 1972. *The Archaeology of Knowledge*. Smith, A., trans. New York: Pantheon.

_____. 1973. *The Birth of the Clinic: An Archaeology of Medical Perception*. Smith, A., trans. New York: Pantheon.

_____. 1977a. *Discipline and Punish: The Birth of the Prison*. Sheridan, A., trans. New York: Pantheon.

_____. 1977b. *The History of Sexuality, Volume I*. Hurley, R., trans. New York: Pantheon.

_____. 1980. *Power/Knowledge: Selected Interviews and Other Writings*. Gordon, C., ed. New York: Pantheon.

Frankenstein, M. 1992. "Critical Mathematics Education: An Application of Paulo Freire's Epistemology." In Weiler, K and Mitchell,

K., eds., *What Schools Can Do: Critical Pedagogy and Practice.* New York: State University of New York Press.

Freire, P. 1970. *Pedagogy of the Oppressed.* Rámos, M., trans. New York: Continuum.

————. 1985. *Politics of Education.* South Hadley: Bergin & Garvey.

————. 1993. *Education for Critical Consciousness.* New York: Continuum.

————. 1994. *Pedagogy of Hope: Reliving Pedagogy of the Oppressed.* New York: Continuum.

Freire, P. & Faundez, A. 1992. *Learning to Question: A Pedagogy of Liberation.* New York: Continuum.

Freire, P. & Horton, M. 1990. *We Make the Road By Walking: Conversations on Education and Social Change.* Bell, B., Gaventa, J., and Peters, J., eds. Philadelphia: Temple University Press.

Freire, P. & Macedo, D. 1987. *Literacy: Reading the Word and the World.* Massachusetts: Bergin & Garvey.

Freire, P. and Macedo, D. 1998. *Teachers as Cultural Workers: Letters for Those Who Dare Teach.* Boulder: Westview.

Gee, J. 1990. *Social Linguistics and Literacies: Ideology and Discourses.* London: Falmer.

Gilmore, W. 1984. *The Grenada Intervention: Analysis and Documentation.* London: Mansell.

Giroux, H. 1983. *Theory and Resistance in Education: A Pedagogy for the Opposition.* South Hadley: Bergin & Garvey.

————. 1984. "Ideology, Agency, and the Process of Schooling." In Barton, L. and Walker, S., eds. *Social Crisis and Educational Research.* London: Croom and Helm.

————. 1988. *Teachers as Intellectuals: Toward a Critical Pedagogy of Learning.* Westport: Bergin & Garvey.

————. 1992. *Border Crossings: Cultural Workers and the Politics of Education.* New York: Routledge.

————. 1994. *Disturbing Pleasures: Learning Popular Culture.* New York: Routledge.

————. 1997. *Pedagogy and the Politics of Hope: Theory, Culture and Schooling.* Boulder: Westview.

Giroux, H. and McLaren, P. 1992. "Writing from the Margins: Geographies of Identity, Pedagogy, and Power. *Journal of Education* 174: 7-30.

Gore, J. M. 1993. *The Struggle for Pedagogies: Critical and Feminist Discourses as Regimes of Truth.* New York: Routledge.

Gramsci. A. 1971. *Selections from the Prison Notebooks.* Medea, Q. and Smith, N., eds. and trans. London: Lawrence and Wishart.

Gutierrez, K. 1991. "The Effects of Writing Process Instruction on Latino Children." Paper presented at the Annual Meeting of the American Educational Research Association. Chicago, Illinois.

_____. 1992. "A Comparison of Instructional Contexts in Writing Process Classrooms with Latino Children." *Education and Urban Society* 24: 244-262.

_____. 1994. "How Talk, Context, and Script Shape Contexts for Learning: A Cross-Case Comparison of Journal Sharing." *Linguistics and Education* 5: 335-365.

Gutierrez, K. and Larson, J. 1994. "Language Borders: Recitation as Hegemonic Discourse." *International Journal of Educational Reform* 3: 22-36.

Gutierrez, K., Rymes, B. and Larson, J. 1995. "James Brown vs. Brown vs. Board of Education: Script, Counterscript and Underlife in the Classroom." (Original manuscript.) *Harvard Educational Review* 65: 445-471.

Gutierrez, K., Stone, L. and Larson, J. In Press. "Hypermediating in the Urban Classroom: When Scaffolding Becomes Sabotage in Narrative Activity." In Baker, C., Cook-Gumperz, J. and Luke, A., eds., *Literacy and Power*. Oxford: Blackwell.

Hall, S. 1981. "Cultural Studies: Two Paradigms." In Bennett, et al., eds. *Culture, Ideology, and Social Process*. London: Batsford Academic & Educational.

_____. 1986. "Gramsci's Relevance for the Study of Race and Ethnicity." *Journal of Communication Inquiry* 10: 45-60.

_____. 1992. "Cultural Studies and Its Theoretical Legacies." In Grossberg, L. Nelson, C. and Treichler, P., eds. *Cultural Studies*. New York: Routledge.

Halliday, M. 1978. *Language as a Social Semiotic*. London: Edward Arnold.

Hickling-Hudson, A. 1988. "Toward Communication Praxis: Reflections on the Pedagogy of Paulo Freire and Educational Change in Grenada." *Journal of Education* 170: 9-38.

Hirsch, E. D. 1987. *Cultural Literacy: What Every American Needs to Know*. New York: Vintage Books.

Hirshon, S. and Butler, J. 1983. *And Also Teach Them to Read*. Westport: Lawerence Hill.

Holub, R. 1992. *Antonio Gramsci: Beyond Marxism and Postmodernism*. London: Routledge.

Horkheimer, M. 1940. "The Authoritarian State." *TELOS* #27.

_____. 1947. *Eclipse of Reason*. New York: Oxford University Press.

Ivanic, R. and Simpson, J. 1992. "Who's Who in Academic Writing?" In Fairclough, N., ed., *Critical Language Awareness*. New York: Longman.

Janks, H. and Ivanic, R. 1992. "Critical Language Awareness and Emancipatory Discourse." In Fairclough, N., ed., *Critical Language Awareness*. New York: Longman.

Jules, D. 1993. "The Challenge of Popular Education in the Grenada Revolution." In Lankshear, C. and McLaren, P., eds., *Critical Literacy: Politics, Praxis, and the Postmodern*. New York: State University of New York Press.

Karliner, J. N. and Faber, D. 1986. *Nicaragua: An Environmental Perspective*. San Francisco: The Environmental Project on Central America & Food First Books.

Kincheloe, J. 1985. "Using Primary Research to Teach Elementary School Social Studies Methods: Exploring Shreveport's Water." *Social Studies 76*.

_____. 1988. "Community Involvement in Social Studies." *Education Digest 54*.

_____. 1989. "Building Strong Academic Backgrounds for Teachers." *Education Digest 55*.

_____. 1990. "Meta-Analysis, Memory and the Politics of the Past: Historical Method, Curriculum and Social Responsibility." *Social Science Record 27*: 31-39.

_____. 1991. "Educational Historiographical Meta-analysis: Rethinking Methodology in the 1990s." *Qualitative Studies in Education 4*: 231-245.

_____. 1993. *Toward a Critical Politics of Teacher Thinking: Mapping the Postmodern*. Westport: Bergin & Garvey.

Kress, G. 1988. *Linguistic Processes in Sociocultural Practice*. Oxford: Oxford University Press.

_____. 1989. "History and Language: Towards a Social Account of Language Change." *Journal of Pragmatics 13*: 445-466.

Kress, G. and Hodge, R. 1979. *Language as Ideology*. London: Routledge.

La Belle, T. J. 1986. *Non-Formal Education in Latin America and the Caribbean: Stability, Reform, or Revolution?* New York: Praeger.

Labov, W. and Fanshel, D. 1977. *Therapeutic Discourse: Psychotherapy as Conversation*. New York: Academic Press.

Laclau, E. and Mouffe, C. 1985. *Hegemony and Socialist Strategy: Towards a Radical Democratic Politics*. London: Verso.

Lappé, F. M. and Medea, B. 1986. *Nicaragua: Give Change a Chance*. San Francisco: Food First Books.

Lave, J. and Wenger, E. 1991. *Situated Learning: Legitimate Peripheral Participation*. Cambridge: Cambridge University Press.

Luke, A. 1995. "Text and Discourse in Education: An Introduction to Critical Discourse Analysis." In Apple, M., ed., *Review of Research in Education* 21. Washington, D.C.: American Educational Research Association.

Luke, C. and Gore, J., 1992, eds. *Feminisms and Critical Pedagogy*. New York: Routledge.

Lyotard, J. 1984. "An Interview." *Theory, Culture, and Society* 5: 277-310.

_____. 1989. *The Lyotard Reader*. Benjamin, A., ed. London: Basil Blackwell.

Marcuse, H. 1964. *One Dimensional Man*. Boston: Beacon.

_____. 1987 [1932]. *Ontology and the Theory of Historicity*. Benhabib, S., trans. Cambridge: MIT Press.

Marx, K. 1963. *Early Writings*. Bottomore, T., ed. New York: McGraw-Hill.

Marx, K. and Engels, F. 1972. *The Marx-Engels Reader*. Tucker, R., ed. New York: Norton.

Mayo, P. 1994. "Synthesizing Gramsci and Freire: Possibilities for a Theory of Radical Adult Education." *International Journal of Lifelong Education*, 13: 125-148.

Mckenzie, M. 1992. "'What I've Always Known but Never Been Told': Euphemisms, School Discourse, and Empowerment." In Fairclough, N., ed., *Critical Language Awareness*. New York: Longman.

McLaren, P. 1997. *Revolutionary Multiculturalism: Pedagogies of Dissent for the New Millennium*. Boulder: Westview.

_____. 1986. *Schooling as a Ritual Performance: Towards a Political Economy of Educational Symbols and Gestures*. London: Routledge.

_____. 1989. *Life in Schools: An Introduction to Critical Pedagogy in the Foundations of Education*. New York: Longman.

_____. 1992. "Collisions with Otherness: Multiculturalism, the Politics of Difference, and the Ethnographer as Nomad." *American Journal of Semiotics* 2: 121-148.

_____. 1994a. "Multiculturalism and Moral Panic: Critical Pedagogy and the Promotion of Unsettling Literacies." *Voices* 3: 1-11.

_____. 1994b. "Rasquachismo and Critical Pedagogy in the Age of Global Capitalism." Paper presented at the annual convention of the American Educational Research Association. New Orleans, Louisiana.

_____ . 1994c. "Critical Pedagogy, Political Agency, and the Pragmatics of Justice: The Case of Lyotard." *Educational Theory*, 44: 319-340.

_____ . 1995. *Critical Pedagogy and Predatory Culture: Oppositional Politics in a Postmodern Era*. London: Routledge.

_____ . 1997. *Revolutionary Multiculturalism: Pedagogies of Dissent for the New Millennium*. Boulder: Westview.

McLaren, P. and Fischman, G. In Press. "Reclaiming Hope: Teacher Education and Social Justice in the Age of Globalization." *Teacher Education Quarterly*.

McLaren, P., Fischman, G., Serra, S. and Antelo, E. Winter, 1998. "The Specters of Gramsci: Revolutionary Praxis and the Committed Intellectual." Original Manuscript. *Journal of Thought*.

McNeil, J. 1985. *Curriculum: A Comprehensive Introduction*. Boston : Little Brown.

Miller, J. 1993. *The Passion of Michel Foucault*. New York : Simon & Schuster.

Morrow, R. and Torres, C. 1995. *Social Theory and Education: A Critique of Theories of Social and Cultural Reproduction*. New York: State University of New York Press.

Ochs, E. 1993. "Constructing Social Identity: A Language Socialization Perspective." *Research on Language and Social Interaction* 26: 287-306.

O'Hanlon, R. 1988. "Recovering the Subject: Subaltern Studies and Histories of Resistance in Colonial South Asia." *Modern Asian Studies* 22: 222-233.

Pêcheux, M. 1982. *Language, Semantics and Ideology*. London: MacMillan.

Potter, J. and Wetherell, M. 1987. *Discourse and Social Psychology: Beyond Attitudes and Behavior*. London: Sage.

Pruyn, M. 1992. "Implementing the Freirean Model Under Siege: Literacy Campaigns in El Salvador, Grenada, and Nicaragua." An unpublished paper. University of California, Los Angeles.

_____ . 1994a. "Becoming Subjects Through Critical Practice: How an Elementary Classroom Critically Read And Wrote Their World." *International Journal of Educational Reform* 3: 37-50.

Pruyn, M. and Fischman, G. 1998. "'*De Nosotros Sale Nada*': The Social Construction of Literacy in a Critically Informed Adult Spanish Literacy Classroom." In Steinberg, S. and Kincheloe, J, eds. *Multicultural Conversations*. New York: Peter Lang.

Puiggrós, A. 1983. "Discuciónes y Tendencias en la Educación Popular Latino-Americana." *Nueva Antropología* 6: 15-39.

_____. 1986. *La Educación Popular en America Latina, 2.* México, D.F.: Secretaría de Educación Pública.

Ravitch, D. 1990. "Diversity and Democracy: Multicultural Education in America." *American Educator* 14: 16-20.

_____. 1991. A culture in common. *Educational Leadership*, 49(4), 8-11.

Sacks, H. 1972. "1967-1971: Mimeo Lecture Notes. On the Analyzability of Stories of Children." In Gumpers, J. and Hymes, D., eds., *Directions in Sociolinguistics.* New York: Holt, Rinehart & Winston.

Sacks, H., Jefferson, G., and Schegloff, E. 1977. "The Preference for Self-correction of Repairs in Conversation." *Language* 53: 361-362.

Sacks, H., Schegloff, E. and Jefferson, G. 1974. "A Simplest Systematics for the Organization of Turn-Taking In Conversation." *Language* 50: 696-735.

Shor, I. 1993. "Education is Politics: Paulo Freire's Critical Pedagogy." In McLaren, P. and Leonard, P., eds., *Paulo Freire: A Critical Encounter.* New York: Routledge.

Shor, I. and Freire, P. 1987. *A Pedagogy for Liberation: Dialogues on Transforming Education.* Massachusetts: Bergin & Garvey.

Sinclair, J. and Coulthard, M. 1975. *Towards an Analysis of Discourse: The English Used by Teachers and Pupils.* Oxford: Oxford University Press.

Spener, D. 1990. "The Freirean Approach to Adult Literacy Education." Eric document #DE321615, National Clearinghouse on Literacy, Washington, D. C.

Torres, C. A. 1990. *The Politics of Non-Formal Education in Latin America.* New York: Praeger.

_____. 1991. "The State, Non-Formal Education, and Socialism in Cuba, Nicaragua, and Grenada." *Comparative Education Review* 35: 110-130.

_____. 1994. "Literacy and Critical Modernism." *International Journal of Educational Reform* 3: 51-52.

Torrez, M. 1986. *Educación Popular: Un Encuentro con Paulo Freire.* Quinto: Corporación Ecuatoriana para el Desarrollo de la Comunicación.

Usher, R. and Edwards, R. 1994. *Postmodernism and Education.* London: Routledge.

Vázquez-Camarena, I. 1987. "'Dawn of the People': The Nicaraguan Literacy Crusade." An unpublished paper, California State University, Los Angeles.

Weiler, K. 1988. *Women Teaching for Change: Gender, Class and Power.* South Hadley: Bergin & Garvey.

_____ . 1991. "Freire and a Feminist Pedagogy of Difference." *Harvard Educational Review* 61: 449-474.

_____ . 1997. "Reflections on Writing a History of Women Teachers." *Harvard Educational Review* 66: 635-657.

Weiler, K. and Mitchell, C., eds., 1992. *What Schools Can Do: Critical Pedagogy and Practice*. New York: State University of New York.

Willis, P. 1977. *Learning to Labour*. Lexington: D. C. Heath.

Wright, E. O. 1978. *Class, Crisis and the State*. London: NLB.

Wright, E. O., Levine, A., and Sober, E. 1992. *Reconstructing Marxism: Essays on Explanation and the Theory of History*. London: Verso.

Zaretsky, E. 1994. "Identity Theory, Identity Politics: Psychoanalysis, Marxism, Post-Structuralism." In Calhoun, C., ed. *Social Theory and the Politics of Identity*. Oxford: Blackwell.

Contextualizing the Study
en la Vida Cotidiana

Refugee road, refugee road
Where do I go from here?
Weary my feet! Heavy the road!
My heart is filled with fear.

—Langston Hughes ("Song of the Refugee Road")

The goal of this chapter will be to elaborate the specific sociocultural, historical, methodological and personal contexts at the heart of this qualitative study of critical student agency conducted in the Central American and Mexican refugee community of Los Angeles. The driving theoretical and inquisitive imperative, the *rason d'être*, behind this work, is a desire to understand the social and discursive practices of this one critically-inspired classroom, and how these practices either advanced or hindered the Freirean/liberatory objectives that were its goal. With this in mind, a description of the research site, its goals, and its participants will follow.

A Community-Based Research Project

Niños color de mi tierra,
Con sus mismas cicatrices
Millonarios de lombrices
Y por eso,
Que triste viven los niños en las casas de cartón

—"Casas de Cartón"

Siempre Adelante,[1] "Always Forward," is a progressive, community-based solidarity organization that serves a predominantly

Salvadoran, Guatemalan and Mexican political and economic refugee community in Los Angeles. The organization offers a host of services to the local community. They provide legal advice, free of charge, on issues including immigration, residency and citizenship; collect and distribute food and other necessities to poor families in the neighborhood; and offer recreational and self-defense classes for children. Additionally, this non-profit group works in and with various political movements advocating immigrant rights; compiles and distributes information on the political situations, the economies, and human rights assessments in El Salvador, Guatemala and México; and provides ESL and Spanish literacy classes, at no cost, to interested adults in the community. *Siempre* receives its revenue from fund raising events throughout the city and from foundation grants and other sources.

These services are crucial to the political and economic survival of the recently immigrated Central American community specifically, and the larger Latina/o community more generally, in Los Angeles—especially given current demographic and political trends in the city and state.

As of 1985, it was estimated that sixty million adults in the United States—one out of every three—was illiterate (Kozol 1985). More specifically, approximately twenty million adults could not read or write at all, and nearly forty million had literacy skills at or below the fifth grade level. Today, while the number of *absolute* illiterates has fallen, the number of *functional* illiterates has dramatically increased. A 1993 government study showed the number of illiterates at over eighty million, half the adult population of the country (*Reading Today*, 1993). This effectively implies the political and economic disenfranchisement of millions of North Americans. Individuals who do not have complete facility in reading and writing "standard" English are disenfranchised from forms of political and economic participation that might economically or politically advantage them.

While European American native English speakers comprise the bulk of those adults who cannot read and write, illiteracy is still unevenly distributed in the United States. So-called "minority" or "special interest" groups (immigrants, non-native English speakers, Latinos, African Americans, Asian Americans, women and the working class) make-up a disproportionate number of the illiterate population when compared to the figures found in society as a whole (Kozol 1985; *Reading Today* 1993). These illiteracy rates are a hindrance (at best) and an impenetrable barrier (at worst), when looking at parents' ability to work with and assist their school-aged children in the development of their literacy. Illiteracy therefore tends to be generational, thus continuing to disproportionately effect people of color, women and the working class.

Institutionalized racism and classism (Los Angeles Unified School District 1990; Oakes 1985) have also had devastating effects on the progress of children of color in our public schools, especially Latino and African American youth. A 1993 report by the Tomás Rivera Center (Darder, Ingle & Cox) detailed the particularly grim state of affairs for the 6.25 million Latina/o children in the public schools of the United States, a majority of whom live in California:

- More Latina/o youth drop out of high school than do youth from any other ethnic group;
- Nearly twelve percent of Latinas/os over twenty-five years old never finished fifth grade;
- Only fifty-three percent complete high school;
- From those who do graduate, only forty-five percent enter college; and,
- Fewer than ten percent of Latinas/os over twenty-five years of age have received a bachelor's degree.

Darder, Ingle & Cox (1993) note:

Only forty-two percent of today's Latino students have parents who are high school graduates. Moreover, forty-three percent have parents with less than nine years of schooling. Lower parent educational attainment levels generally mean lower income; both factors correlate with lower levels of success among children. Being Latino, living in poverty, and coming to school from an undereducated family dramatically increases the probability of dropping out. (2)

Thus, not surprisingly, illiteracy in the city of Los Angeles, with its large Latina/o and "minority" populations, is a pervasive phenomenon. While many social indicators show that it is currently a difficult time for minorities in general, recent events in California indicate that times are even *more* difficult, and potentially oppressive, for Latinas/os (among others). Proposition 187, passed by a minority of Californians in 1994, while dressed-up as a law seeking only to save the state resources unnecessarily expended on "aliens" who are "illegally" residing within the state, was really a thinly veiled attack on the state's Latina/o workers. This initiative, put on the ballot and funded by White supremacist groups,[2] sought to attack the state's undocumented workers despite that fact that these same workers helped keep California's economy afloat during the state's recent recession/depression by working for sub-minimum wages while drawing little or no social services—beyond education for their children and emergency medical care—all of which they more than made-up for with the consumption taxes they regularly paid.

The year 1996 witnessed two further social attacks aimed not only at Latinas/os, but at other people of color, and at women. First, the Regents of the University of California voted to abolish affirmative action in student admissions and faculty hiring,[3] thus reversing a policy that had been making slow but steady progress over the past two decades in increasing the percentages of traditionally underrepresented groups among the student and faculty populations. Second, California voters[4] continued the legal onslaught against people of color (and now women), begun in 1994 with Proposition 187, by passing proposition 209, the speciously titled "California Civil Rights Initiative." This new law disallows all affirmative action in dealings with the state of California that pertain to public education, employment and contracts. Most recently (June 1998), the voters of California passed Proposition 227, the so-called, "English for the Children" Initiative, which would virtually do away with all bilingual education programs for the State's non-English speaking school children. This triumvirate of reactionary law in California is expected to adversely effect the already burdened Latina/o population of the state educationally, economically and politically.

It is within this pedagogical and sociopolitical context that the community-based organization at the center of this study, and the educational program they offered, sought alternatives to the failures of the public school system in educating Latinas/os; in this case, through the model of "popular education."

When I learned that *Siempre,* a group whose work I had always admired and supported, had begun a Freirean-inspired popular education program to bring Spanish literacy and English fluency to the neighborhood where they were based, my interest was piqued. In particular, I became interested in studying this program because of its stated emphasis on the development of students' critical consciousness and agency. Having long had an interest in the potential of Freirean pedagogy and practice, I soon found myself planning and implementing a qualitative investigation in their intermediate Spanish literacy classroom with the full, if not curious, support of the students and teacher. The present study, which centers on the experiences of this one classroom of Spanish literacy students, grew out of that initial investigation. This study focuses on the instructional and social practices of three teachers, Guillermo, Daisy and Nadia, and their one group of consecutively shared students, over a thirteen month period. As events played themselves out at this site, I found evolving before me a rich comparative case study of critical student agency. The two primary stated goals of the ESL/literacy project within which the intermediate Spanish literacy classroom was situated were to develop literacy skills and to foster techniques for critical reflection—that is, analysis and action (agency)—within their students.[5]

The Students

Through interviews with the adult learners in this classroom, it became clear that they had been socialized *to use* language, and *through* language (Ochs 1988), in very traditional ways during their earlier educational experiences in Central America and Mexico. Those who had received some formal schooling in their native countries reported that their former teachers had used what Freire describes as a "banking" model of teaching and learning. Under this highly restrictive, teacher-centered pedagogical approach, the teacher creates and transmits knowledge, while students are to assume the role of passive receivers of this knowledge. Under this hegemonic pedagogical model, students are seen as *passive* social/historical subjects (or even "objects"), instead of *active* social/historical subjects who can create their own forms of meaning (Freire 1970; McLaren 1989).

While a majority of the students had had some form of previous schooling, nearly one third of the students had received no formal schooling at all in their countries of origin, or as adults in the United States. For those students who had received some formal schooling, their educational careers were short in duration. For example, Fernando (who will figure prominently in the social practices of Nadia's classroom in Chapter 6), reported attending school in rural Mexico until the age of ten. Because he was the oldest of several children in the family, Fernando's parents informed him—on his tenth birthday—that he was needed at home, where he would work with his mother and father in tending the small parcel of land they farmed. Additionally, his mother told him, it was necessary for him to work so that his younger siblings could also have the opportunity to receive some schooling. After all, Fernando's parents reminded him, he had had the opportunity to attend school through the fourth grade—a big accomplishment. As he shared this story with me some nineteen years later in Los Angels, he seemed to harbor no ill will toward his parents for their decision. This was the way it was done.

So for these students, their experiences in this Freirean-inspired classroom were quite unique. Of the two thirds of the students who had attended school at all, even if for only a short period, they had only been exposed to banking/hegemonic pedagogy. And for the rest of the students, this was their very first formal introduction to literacy instruction, "critical" or otherwise.

More detailed descriptions of the students will be presented in Chapters 4, 5 and 6. In these descriptions, there will be a special emphasis placed on those students whose social practices were most representative of the class as a whole.

During this year-long study, these adult learners worked with three very distinct teachers: Guillermo, Daisy and Nadia. To understand the social practices that informed these students' attempts to gain literacy skills, and the program's attempts to develop critical student agency within them, we must first understand the implicit and explicit philosophical and pedagogical theories that guided their teachers' practice. These three teachers, their pedagogical orientations, and the circumstances that placed them in this classroom of learners, are detailed in the following section.

Guillermo Linares, Daisy Contreras
and Nadia Monterey: The Three Teachers

Guillermo Linares, the students' first teacher, had taught grades kindergarten through eight for fifteen years in his native El Salvador before moving to Los Angeles. He reported being forced to leave his country as a result of his leftist and pro-human rights political views and activities. Guillermo was in his mid-thirties, was soft spoken, and always seemed to be smiling. As the teacher of the intermediate Spanish literacy class at *Siempre Adelante*, Guillermo told me he did not get paid very well, especially given the cost of living in Los Angeles. He said he understood, however, in that *Siempre* is a non-profit organization funded by grants, and does not have a very large budget. To make ends meet, Guillermo worked part-time as a "stock boy" at a local electronics store, and shared his one bedroom apartment with two roommates. He said he made this sacrifice, and stayed at *Siempre*, because he loved teaching and wanted to make a difference in his students' lives. During a teacher training session, Guillermo shared that he saw the role of the teacher as being one of "bringing consciousness to those in our care." In early October of 1993—four months into my formal collection of data in his classroom—Guillermo quit his teaching post. During an interview several days later, he shared his reasons for leaving, "I don't get along with Daisy...Besides, it's hard to work two jobs. And it's hard to work at night."

Daisy Contreras was Guillermo's boss. She and Guillermo had been at odds since she joined the organization as the coordinator of the ESL and Spanish literacy program shortly after I began collecting data in June of 1993. On several occasions, Guillermo lost his temper at Daisy in front of students, and he regularly spoke negatively about her to his colleagues. During an informal discussion with Daisy in mid-October, she shared that she felt Guillermo left because he did not want to change his "hierarchical" and "authoritarian" ways of teaching and being with students. She thought that Guillermo did not want to adapt to the Freirean/critical teaching philosophy under which the program was founded, and which she had been encouraging in on-going teacher training sessions.

Daisy asked me if I could come in and substitute for Guillermo on the day after he left. I agreed. That evening, Guillermo's students and I talked about his departure. One student, Gloria, shared that she did not like Guillermo, that he was "mean." Several of the other students agree, yet expressed ambivalence about his departure. Later that evening, during the break, another of Guillermo's students, Farabundo, told me, "Our teacher left us." When I asked him how it made him feel, he simply responded, "He said he didn't want to leave us, but he left us." Farabundo appeared genuinely sad.[6] The next day, Daisy took over as interim substitute until a permanent replacement could be found. She taught the class for the next two months.

Daisy, born, trained and having worked as a teacher in Argentina, was in here late-twenties. After coming to Los Angeles, Daisy's goals were to pursue graduate study in education or urban planning, and to gain new experiences—in a North American context—working within the city's politically-oriented non-profit organizations as a grass-roots organizer. While she was in Los Angeles, she worked for *Siempre Adelante*, a trade union and a women's organization—predominately focusing on educational work. She has since returned to Latin America and is now working on a multi-million dollar international critical literacy program with indigenous women. Her teacher training, and early classroom practice, were similar to Guillermo's. This training focused on phonics instruction, the syllabic approach to teaching literacy, and teacher-centered pedagogies—as has been the case in most teacher education programs throughout the world. Yet it was reported that her larger personal commitment to confronting socio-political conflicts and authoritarianism within Argentina, from a perspective of social change and empowerment, forced her to also begin challenging and problematizing her own traditional socialization as a teacher. Over time, this led her to formulate a very different perspective on student-teacher social practices and classroom power relations than she was taught. She told me that for her, the goal of education, especially in non-formal settings such as this one, should be to give students the kind of analytical and political tools that will help them transform problematic socioeconomic conditions in their lives.

Through comments she made at teacher training sessions, it appeared that she theoretically grounded her community work in a Freirean/critical/popular philosophy, and in neo- and postmodern Marxism. On one occasion, Daisy shared with me that she saw the political and consciousness-raising work of the ESL/literacy project as even more important that the pedagogical work. She said that if classroom activities were based on students' economic and social lives here in Los Angeles, and on the project of improving them, then learning would naturally follow. For Daisy, this development of critical consciousness and critical student agency did not necessarily have to manifest in large-scale political action to be significant, to be important. She commented that, "Sometimes actions are small, step-by-step, determined by the group. The day-by-day stuff, to have a voice, this is political. To me, this is transformational." So for Daisy, even small classroom manifestations of critical awareness and agency counted and were important.

Throughout the month of December 1993, Daisy intensified her search for a permanent replacement for Guillermo. By the end of the month, she found a new Spanish literacy teacher, Miguel Osorio. Miguel was young, enthusiastic and outwardly committed to *Siempre's* Freirean-inspired approach. Instead of handing Guillermo's former students directly over to Miguel, however, Daisy thought it advisable to evaluate all of the Spanish literacy students, and possibly consider a reorganization of the two classes. Daisy had been teaching the intermediate class, and Nadia Monterey had been teaching the beginning group (they had no "advanced" group at that time). The students were assessed by Daisy and Nadia (I was asked for my input as well), and two new classes were reorganized based on ability level: "*Alfa*[7] 1" (the more novice group) and "*Alfa* 2" (the more advanced group). A majority of Guillermo and Daisy's former students moved into the *Alfa* 2 group, which was to be taught by Nadia. Miguel was given the *Alfa* 1 group. Most of the students that had been the focus of this study then found themselves working with Nadia, their third teacher in seven months.

Nadia Monterey, who was in her late thirties, was very personable and outgoing. She was born in El Salvador, where she worked as both a classroom teacher and school principal. Nadia came to live in Los Angeles to be with family members who had already emigrated from El Salvador, and for economic reasons of her own, although she had begun to find economic and political life in Los Angeles more difficult than she thought she would. Nadia shared with me that she was doing this job for the income, meager though it was. Although she said she loved teaching, Nadia would have rather been spending her evenings attending ESL classes as a student to "improve herself," rather than teaching a Spanish literacy class. To bring in extra income, for herself and her fourteen-year-old son, she also cared for young children out of her home during the day. Eventually, Nadia expressed, she would like to be a licensed teacher in this country.

One very refreshing trait about Nadia was her honesty and openness. She was as quick to share her strengths and weaknesses as a teacher as she was to share her feelings about the Freirean-oriented program in which she worked. For example, Nadia said she did not know how to print very well, so she had to put everything in handwriting. "You could probably teach *me*," she confided with a smile and laugh. Philosophically and pedagogically, Nadia shared, "We need a method. In the end, all teachers have something to 'give' to students." She continued, "I don't teach the names and sounds of the letters, just the sounds of the syllables. It's called the 'phonetic method'."

She was considered a "traditionalist" by Daisy and some of her other colleagues because of her frequently expressed doubts about Freirean pedagogy, and her preference for "phonics" and "skills-based" instruction.[8] During the program's frequent teacher training sessions, Nadia often openly shared her concerns with the Freirean approach to teaching. "I agree with conscientization," she commented, "but my first objective is that my students know the vowels...We should teach the syllables first, then generate words."

It is with these three teachers, and the classroom discourse communities they helped to create, that the group of students in this study found themselves. The following section details the types of data that were collected for this study and the forms of collection used to gather those data.

Windows on the Site: The Data

The data for this study were collected over an exhilarating, nerve-racking and intellectually stimulating period beginning in early summer of 1993 and ending a little over a year later. During my fifty-six weeks of ethnographic field work, the adult literacy students in the classroom changed teachers three times. Additionally, there was a program-wide classroom reorganization half-way through data collection that shifted some students away and added several newcomers to the classroom under observation. Further, during the course of data collection, the literacy/ESL program experienced a change in venue and a major facilities renovation. This was challenging for all involved. My "travails" as researcher, however, hardly compared to those of the students in the program, who were already burdened with trying to get to the two hour class sessions four nights a week while at the same time holding down a job or two to maintain economic viability in recession-choked Los Angeles of 1993 and 1994.

I chose an ethnographic case study methodology for this study. I did so not only because what I encountered in the field was a naturally occurring, on-going case, but also because these methods allowed me to *contextualize* the social interactions I observed at the research site (Walcott 1988), which was one of my primary objectives. Qualitative research generally, and case study methodology in particular, allow us as researchers to access simultaneously the micro *and* macro processes within social interactions that comprise phenomena within educational and other settings (Miles & Huberman 1984; Oakes, Gamoran & Page 1992). This was especially important in a study like this, where critical discourse analysis was used. Further, these methods can help us see how participants construct understandings for themselves as they participate in their everyday experiences at a given research site. This was key to my goal of understanding how students' critical agentive skills and identities were formed as they participated in the literacy practices of the classroom. My use of case study methods allowed me to look at the real life change processes as they occurred naturally over time at *Siempre* (Yin 1984). For the purposes of this study, a study whose goal is to unpackage both micro and macro social phenomena within one educational setting, there was no other choice, for practical or theoretical reasons, than to use case study research methods.

The wide range of data I collected at *Siempre* included field notes of classroom sessions, teacher trainings, school-sponsored parties, fund raisers, and internal and external political events. They also included audio-taped interviews with students, teachers, program coordinators, directors, the executive director and former teachers and coordinators. Additionally, audio- and video-tapes of classroom sessions, special events and teacher trainings were gathered. Archival documents such as project funding proposals and evaluations, internal program reviews, teachers' unit and lesson plans, training documents, student workbooks, and flyers produced by the ESL/literacy project and *Siempre* helped to round-out the study's corpus of data.

It was my hope that these different types of data would allow for an examination of the discursive social practices of this group of students at the micro, mid-range and macro level. It was my expectation that the audio- and video-taped data would provide a window into the micro-discursive practices; the field notes and interviews into the mid-range discursive practices; and the archival and documentary data into the macro-discursive practices of this evolving classroom. Additionally, these multiple data sources allowed for triangulation of findings (Strauss & Corbin 1994).

A brief note on the dominant language of the classroom, of the organization and of the researcher, and how it effected data collection, is in order here. Spanish, as might be assumed, was the primary language used in this *Spanish* literacy class, as well as during teacher trainings and at most social/political events and gatherings sponsored my the organization. As an English/Spanish bilingual researcher, while taking field notes, I would translate what I heard and observed directly into English as I wrote it down my notes. If I was unsure of the meaning of a word or phrase, I would note it down in Spanish for future consultation with my trusted collection of Spanish/English-English/Spanish dictionaries and other bilingual colleagues. This was the most efficient way I found of dealing with the translation issue. Many of the classroom and training sessions were also audio- and/or video-taped. This allowed me to double check my translation where and if necessary. It also allowed me to do detailed discursive (verbal and gestural) transcriptions of key representative classroom interactions. However, in a number of instances, my on-the-spot translated field notes were the primary and only form of data I had available as data analysis progressed. So, for many examples, the data presented in this book will be in English. When possible however, both the original Spanish version, as well as the translated English version, will be provided. The dual Spanish/English transcription will be most evident when data from Nadia's classroom is presented in Chapter 6, for it was in her classroom that I was allowed to video tape most extensively.

The Foci of Analyses

There are two foci that helped to direct my analyses of the data collected for this study, one general and one more specific. Generally, I began analyzing the data by focusing on classroom literacy practices and instruction—at the midrange and microinteractional level—with special attention to literacy activities. I asked questions to myself and of the data such as: When are the students engaged in "literacy practices"? When are they *dis*engaged? When does it appear that the teacher is attempting to provide "instruction"? When does it appear that she or he is not? What do "literacy activities" within this setting look like? What do they not look like? Asking and attempting to answer these questions—with much personal reflection and consultation with colleagues and the literature (and then further reflection!)—aided me in beginning to organize my hundreds of pages of field notes and my many hours of audio- and video-taped classroom sessions and interviews.

This, while helpful, led of course, to more questions: *Why* were students at times engaged and at other times not engaged during classroom literacy practices? During teacher instruction? This was a helpful tool and line of inquiry. For my attempt at answering these questions, see Chapters 4, 5 and 6, where I use a critical discourse analysis inspired by Gramsci (1971), Foucault (1977a), Freire (1970; Freire & Macedo 1987), McLaren (1989, 1997) and Fairclough (1992a) to understand and try to explain how and why gaps and slippages in the literacy practices and the teacher's instruction existed; that is, how and why students conformed, resisted or acted agentively against any given set of classroom practices.

But as analyses proceeded, I found I needed a unit of analysis even more specific than that of "literacy activities" or "literacy instruction," *per se*. So I turned to the teacher/student "initiation-response-evaluation" (IRE) discourse pattern—the predominate interactional pattern in teacher-centered classrooms. The way in which I conceived of and operationalized this IRE pattern was most significantly informed by the work of Gutierrez (1991a, 1992, 1994). Gutierrez notes that the IRE discourse pattern is formed when the teacher initiates an interaction, the student(s) responds and the teacher evaluates that response.[9] The following is an example of the IRE discourse pattern:

Kris:	Marc, what is the capital of California?	(initiation)	I
Marc:	Sacramento.	(response)	R
Kris:	Correct.	(evaluation)	E

In describing this common interactional sequence, first identified by Mehan (1979), Gutierrez (1992) notes:

> In this discourse pattern, the teacher initiates a question, the student responds to that question, and the teacher follows with an evaluation of that response...Students have minimal opportunities to produce elaborated talk, to generate new ideas, to experiment with their own writing, and to participate in their own meaning-making activities. Instead, students generally have to rely on the teacher or textbooks for new information and assistance. (251)

Strict adherence to this traditional, teacher-centered form of classroom interaction has been associated with "recitation instruction" and the use of a "recitation script" by teachers (Gutierrez 1992, 1994, In Press). Under rigid applications of the IRE discourse pattern, "the nature of the student response is short (one word or phrase)." Indeed, under this form of student-teacher discursive interaction, student responses are often discouraged by the teacher (Gutierrez 1991b:6). These traditional IRE patterns have been shown to foster unequal distributions of power in classrooms and to inhibit the development of academic competencies among students (Gutierrez 1994; Gutierrez & Larson 1994).

The exclusive use of a strict recitation discourse pattern has been shown to have negative social and cognitive consequences on students. However, recitation need not necessarily *always* be equated with negative consequences. Studies of classroom discourse and its relationship to literacy learning have shown that more effective classrooms are characterized by *multiple* scripts[10] or varying patterns of classroom interaction. Moreover, effective teachers use the recitation script sparingly, strategically and purposefully (Gutierrez 1991a, 1992, 1993).

My analyses of this study's data revealed that IRE was a very common and consistent discourse pattern across the practice of all three teachers. But, depending on the teacher with which the students were working, and the nature of the discourse community they had jointly constructed, the IRE pattern alternately appeared rigid and strict in its usage, and at other times more loose. For this reason, the IRE discourse pattern as a unit of analysis was a useful organizational and analytical tool in my investigation of critical student agency across the three different contexts. However, as I began initial analysis of the data, I found that depending on the teacher, there were some variations in the use of IRE. Under the first teacher, Guillermo, the discourse pattern was more one of initiation-response (IR), with the "evaluation" subsumed into the teacher's next initiation. The following example shows how this looks in practice:

1	Kris:	Marc, who wrote	initiation	I
2		*Pedagogy of the Oppressed?*		
3	Marc:	Paulo Freire.	response	R
4	Kris:	And *Culture and Power in the Classroom?*	(implicit evaluation) new initiation	(E)/I
5	Marc:	Antonia Darder.	response	R
6	Kris:	And *Literacy and Power?*	(implicit evaluation) new initiation	(E)/I

Following this example, lines 1-3, and 4-5 represent IR, and not IRE sequences. Yet there *is* an evaluation. It is just implicit.

Under Daisy, the second teacher, more of a traditional IRE discourse pattern was followed—although, as shall be see in Chapter 5, much more loosely. And under the third teacher, Nadia, both IR and IRE patterns were followed. For the purposes of this study, therefore, both IR and IRE discourse patterns will be used as a unit of analysis, depending on how they emerged from the data in each particular setting.

While IRE discourse patterns were central to the analysis of the social practices of this classroom, and the effect these practices had on the development of critical student agency, there were also other levels of analysis. Student interview data and field notes were also analyzed. These other data sources, and layers of analysis, were very helpful in mostly corroborating, but at times challenging, the findings that emerged from the analyses of both the literacy practices and IRE discourse patterns. These will also be explored at some length.

From the Theory and Data: Analytical Codes

The codes that were used to analyze the data from this study represent an interplay between the data that were collected and theoretical framework laid out in the previous chapter. Therefore, each code will be described and operationalized with an eye toward both the theory that informed it, and its emergence in initial and then on-going analyses of the data.

Drawing on a Gramscian definition of agency,[11] and a definition of "critical student agency" as informed by Freirean pedagogy,[12] I conducted a first pass of coding of the data using the categories of student "resistant acts" and "agentive acts." Theoretically, I conceived these to be acts students would engage in in opposition to hegemonic pedagogical practices—especially the agentive acts. Hegemonic pedagogical practices are teacher and student acts which follow the "banking" pedagogy model described by Freire (1970, 1985), and the "recitation" pedagogy model elaborated by Gutierrez (1991a, 1992). Within these hegemonic pedagogical practices, the classroom is a teacher-centered place where information is "transmitted" from the all-knowing teacher to the "empty" students. Classroom practices such as these support the hegemonic order by keeping teachers in positions of authority and power in classrooms and keeping students subordinated to that authority. Because the literacy program at *Siempre Adelante* was Freirean in orientation, I initially expected to observe students developing agentive views of self and beginning to act in opposition to hegemonic pedagogical practices. In other words, I hoped to see manifestations of critical student agency.

This initial coding and analysis of the data *did* reveal categories of student and teacher discursive behaviors that I expected to find. But it also revealed categories of student and teacher behavior I was *not* expecting. First—and as one might have expected—it was not only the students who were taking various discursive actions in the classroom, but the teachers were as well. And I had not originally coded for teacher acts. The data revealed that teachers were discursively "positioning" students in two ways. The teachers either positioned students as active social subjects (discursively placing students in roles where they could co-construct classroom knowledge with the teacher and their classmates) or attempted to position them as the "objects" of instruction (following a hegemonic/banking/recitation model with students as receivers of knowledge). My set of codes evolved as this former set of teacher acts was labeled "student subjectification," and the latter set of teacher acts "student objectification."

Second, what emerged from the data on the part of students were not so much "acts," but "stances," discursive stances that students assumed during classroom literacy activities and within IRE discursive sequences. And while these student stances did assume "resistant" and "agentive" forms at times, as I had expected, they also assumed "conformist" forms. My initial analyses of the data revealed that students were assuming "resistant," "agentive" *and/or "conformist"* stances in relation to dominant hegemonic pedagogical practices, depending on the activity in which they were engaged, and the teacher with which they were working.

In summary, my beginning—and then on-going—analyses of the data indicated that students assumed three different "stances" during IRE discursive sequences: 1) "conformist stances," 2) "resistant stances" and 3) "agentive stances." Further, it was also revealed that teachers attempted to discursively "position" students in two different ways during these and other interactions: either as active social subjects ("student subjectification") or as passive social objects ("student objectification"). All field notes, transcribed interviews, and summarized video data were then re-analyzed in great depth using these revised codes. These more elaborated codes became useful tools, as through them, I was able to identify consistent patterns of student and teacher behaviors across the three different contexts in which these students found themselves (these patterns, and the discourse communities they helped create, are described in detail in Chapters 4, 5 and 6). Based on this re-coding and deeper level of analysis of the data, and in further reflection with the theory that inspired the original codes, I constructed the following elaborated definitions.

Student Conformist Stances

The student assuming a "conformist stance" does not demonstrate observable resistance or opposition to hegemonic pedagogical practices. During their self-positioning in a conformist stance, the student complies with the directives and mandates of the teacher and acts as a "student is supposed to act" under hegemonic pedagogical practices.[13] The data from this study seemed to indicate that while a student acting in this way may occasionally exhibit displeasure with hegemonic practices, they make no observable effort to resist or change these practices. It is often accepted that this is "just the way schooling is." The student is a passive social subject, seen by themselves, and the teacher, as an "object" to be acted upon by the teacher (Freire 1970). As students assume conformist stances, they are positioned, and self-position (Foucault 1977a), through tacit agreement/acquiescence to hegemonic pedagogical practices, as followers. Through these and other micro-social processes, hegemony (Gramsci 1971), and the existing social order, is followed and maintained.

Student Resistant Stances

The student taking a "resistant stance" demonstrates observable resistance to hegemonic pedagogical practices. As the resistant stance is assumed, the student exhibits not only displeasure with hegemonic pedagogical practices, but actually *ignores* and/or *disobeys* directives and mandates from the teacher operating under the hegemonic model—thus going beyond the potential "displeasure" demonstrated under conformism. However, while resistance (often in the form of non-compliance) is offered against hegemonic classroom practices, the "resisting" student does not elaborate a preferable set of counter-hegemonic pedagogical practices, nor act in a concerted way (individually or with other students) to bring about these alternative practices—whether they are conceiving of these possible different forms of action in these words or in others. In this instance, the student may still be being positioned as an "object" acted upon by others (Freire 1970), but is now also attempting to resist this objectification. By assuming resistant stances, students theoretically act-out against their positioning as followers. Yet, according to Gramsci (1971) and Willis (1977) (and I agree with them), resistance alone is not enough to change the hegemonic order. As Gramsci reminds us (1971), resistance involves displaying signs of "subaltern discontent" versus "*conscious efforts*" at social change. Some note (see Willis 1977) that unstrategic and uncoordinated forms of resistance may actually serve to *reinforce* the hegemonic order; while others see resistance as a useful tool of gradual social change (Gore 1993; O'Hanlon 1988). The outcomes of students assuming resistant rather than agentive stances will become clear as the classroom data in the following three chapters is explored.

Student Agentive Stances

The student assuming an "agentive stance" takes action that attempts to alter existing hegemonic pedagogical practices. The student actively engages problematic issues that arise in the curriculum, or in classroom relations with the teacher and/or classmates, and takes some form of action to change them. This student is active, a "subject" acting on the world in order to change it. It is in this way—using Freire's terminology (1970)—that human beings realize their full potential as social subjects. Through agentive stances, students self-position as actors as they struggle against the on-going attempt of hegemonic pedagogical practices to position them as followers. This is one of the main goals of critical pedagogy: to move students from conformism and/or resistance to agency (Freire 1970, 1985, 1997; Freire & Horton 1990; Freire & Macedo 1987, 1998). Agency replaces passive resistance as counter-hegemonic attitudes develop (Gramsci 1971). A student in the midst of assuming an agentive stance elaborates or acts out a preferable set of counter-hegemonic pedagogical practices. Further, this student acts in a concerted way (individually or with other students) to make these alternative and liberating practices central to the practice of the classroom.

Teacher Objectification or Subjectification of Students

I have coded the instances in the data when the teacher attempts to position students as *objects* as "student objectification." Instances where the teacher positions the students as *active social subjects* were coded as "student subjectification.

Data Coding, Organization and Analysis

The data for this study were segmented, coded, organized and analyzed in the following way. First, the these analytical codes had been developed and refined, all of the data were organized into literacy activities. These activities included reading from the board, discussing a theme, taking dictation, copying from the board into notebooks, making a list of words on the board by combining and recombining syllables, reading from photocopied texts, or any other activity involving students engaging in reading or writing, or attempting to read or write. Second, students' literacy activities were organized and coded using the analytical codes described above. Third, literacy activities with similar coding patterns were organized into like groups under each teacher.[14] Fourth, similarly coded and numerically representative literacy activities were then chosen from the classroom of each teacher. Fifth, and finally, these selected literacy activities were broken up into IRE discourse sequences for micro-discursive analysis.

Pilot Study

The study that is the focus of this volume—as well as its guiding theoretical constructs and analytical tools—had its genesis in a more modest pilot study that focused in a general way on the nature of Freirean-inspired teaching and learning in one classroom (also at *Siempre Adelante*). This earlier qualitative exploratory study was designed to study Freirean-inspired practice in a broad sense, and how students developed—or failed to develop—"critical identities." This study also provided an opportunity to "road test" the preliminary analytical categories and tools elaborated at the beginning of the previous section (resistant and agentive "acts" as opposed to discursive "stances"). It allowed me to

MARC PRUYN

ask self-critical questions such as: Is my theoretical framework useful in understanding how students play-out potentially resistant and agentive roles within the classroom? Are my analytical tools helping me to understand the different phenomena that emerged from the data? Could I answer my research questions? Were they "good" questions?

This pilot research process was very instructive. In the course of the study, a focus on the social construction of critical student "identity" changed to an examination of the development of critical student "agency" through the discursive positioning of students. Most notably, my research questions became much more specific and targeted to one central issue, the discursive development of critical student agency. Further, the questions that guided the pilot work were at first quite broad and general—as was probably appropriate at that stage in my research—and dealt with the larger theme of Freirean pedagogy *in situ*. They later became much more focused.

In the pilot study, I found that teacher socialization of students played an important part in the development of critical student agency. As the teacher consistently acted in ways that treated students as "objects" who play a minimal interactive role in the learning process, students soon learned to "discipline" themselves, in a Foucauldian sense, and indeed play-out, and eventually fulfill, these roles. As the teacher acted in ways that treated students as "active social subjects" who were to play a central interactive role in the learning process, students would also begin to play-out these roles. Based on these findings, I was driven to examine concepts that would help me analyze similar social practices in the larger corpus of data in the following and more ambitious study, and also to connect these classroom social practices to larger phenomena in society. As a result, I began to theoretically investigate the role discourse plays in classrooms and how that might assist me on a micro-analytical level, and to explore the literature on "hegemony," "counter-hegemony" and "agency," and assess how it might help my analyses on a macro-analytical level. Additionally, the pilot study gave me the opportunity to experiment with the codes "student resistant act" and "student agentive act" that were previously discussed. While helpful to some extent, these problematic codes posed more questions than they answered. Many classroom actions on the part of students, for example, were neither "resistant" or "agentive." What I learned from this pilot study experience was brought with me to this current study.

Final Comments on the Methodology

Several challenges arose in the course of conducting this study. While I believe it both presents a number of important findings (which will be elaborated in the chapters below), and effectively addresses the research problem presented in the first chapter, it was not conflict-free.

A potential limitation of this study is the fact that the literacy project it sought to describe has ceased to exist, due to lack of funding. This has limited my ability to gather follow-up data, or to contact participants for further interviewing, as questions arose during data reduction and analysis. However, this door was not completely closed. During data collection, I became close with a number of the students, teachers and coordinators in the project, and have maintained varying levels of contact with them since that time. A long-term solution is to hold on-going formal and informal meetings, discussions and interviews between the research team and those who are the focus of the research during the research process. Specifically, I am thinking of the kind of participatory and iterative research heuristics advanced and described by qualitativists such as Lincoln & Guba (1985). This kind of participatory research paradigm would provide a richer collection of data to analyze, and would also come closer to the dialogic and interactional spirit of the Freirean theory that helped to frame the research itself.

A further potential limitation of this study, for me, is its specificity; that is, it was focused on one small group of students and employed a very micro form of analysis. While this specificity aided in turning the study into a manageable project, I am concerned that its contextual situatedness limits what can be gleaned from its findings. My specific interest in this study was to understand how critical student agency was fostered or hindered through social and discursive interactions in one classroom over time and with different teachers. Freirean practice has yet to be extensively examined in quite this way. However, will this study prove helpful to the larger community of criticalists, researchers and practitioners? Or is it too topically (the social construction of student agency) and locally (*one* Freirean-inspired adult Spanish literacy classroom) specific?

I will not be able to answer these question here. I can only address this potential limitation in the following way. First, at least in this instance, the demographic and micro-analytic specificity of the study was unavoidable. The scope of this investigation was limited to the development of critical student agency, and did not necessarily address larger issues of the *viability* of Freirean pedagogy. This could easily be examined by others interested in the effectiveness of Freirean practice (see the section in Chapter 2, "Freirean Pedagogical Practice: Striving For Agency, Creating Change" for a brief summary of several of the many successful instances of attempted Freirean-inspired teaching). Second, one of the major strands of my own research agenda focuses on examining similar phenomena—the social and discursive development of critical student agency—in other settings: among young learners as well as adults, in formal settings as well as informal settings, and in critically-informed and *non*-critically-informed learning environments. Much of my current work involves trying to determine if what I found of significance in this site also exists at other sites and what these collective findings mean for critical and other radical pedagogies. And I can only hope that this study, as well as my on-going research agenda and emphases, will prove useful to educators, theorists and researchers working within the critical tradition.

Finally, there is the issue of the micro-analysis that I employed. While examining classroom discourse at this intensely minute level of verbal and gestural detail could be understood by some a limitation, it can (and, I believe, does) provide us as researchers and criticalists with rich situated understandings of classrooms and the individuals within them.

The next chapter, "Accepting the Word and the World: Accommodating Hegemony," focuses on the Spanish literacy classroom of Guillermo Linares and his adult students. This chapter describes the kinds and nature of social and discursive interactions in which the students and teacher engaged, and what this meant for the development of critical student agency.

Notes

1. To protect participant confidentiality, pseudonyms have been used for the institution, students and teachers described in this study.

2. See the discussion on the groups FAIR and the Pioneer Fund in Pruyn (1994).

3. This action was taken despite massive student protests and acts of civil disobedience at various University of California (UC) campuses, and the lobbying and other efforts of former Chancellor Charles Young at UCLA, and the President of UC.

4. As with Proposition 187, a numerical minority both of eligible and registered voters.

5. As stated by the program coordinators in interviews, and as discovered in the project's founding and other documents.

6. This, despite the fact that Farabundo was the student who most frequently assumed resistant stances against the hegemonic pedagogical practices at the heart of Guillermo's teaching (see, for instance, Example 1, lines 75-76; Example 2, line 9; and Example 3, line 3, in Chapter 4).

7. *Alfa* was short for *alfabetización*, or Spanish "literacy" class.

8. Even though phonics instruction was a prominent component of the approach originally used by Freire in Brazil or in the Nicaraguan project he helped to implement.

9. Other researchers use the variation of "elicitation-response" discourse sequence(s). See Gonzales, et al., 1995, and the on-going work of the "Third International Mathematics and Science Study, Videotape Classroom Study," James Stigler, Principal Investigator.

10. Gutierrez has also identified the existence and use of "responsive" and "responsive-collaborative" scripts in classrooms (Gutierrez 1992, 1993).

11. Purposeful action taken by an individual, or groups of individuals, to facilitate the creation of counter-hegemonic practices and/or institutions.

12. Purposeful action taken by a student, or group of students, to facilitate the creation of counter-hegemonic pedagogical practices.

13. Under hegemonic pedagogical practices, the student accepts the teacher as an unquestioned authority and provider of "facts" and "knowledge," and sees her or himself as a passive "empty vessel" who needs "filling up" by the teacher. This definition draws on Freire's notion of "banking education" (1970, 1985) and Gutierrez' "recitation instruction" (1992, 1993).

14. For example, all of the literacy activities under Guillermo where students assumed predominately conformist stances were put in

one group. Resistant stances were put in another. And agentive stances were put in yet another. All of the literacy activities under Daisy and Nadia were similarly organized.

References

Darder, A., Ingle, Y., Cox, B. 1993. *The Policies and the Promise: The Public School of Latino Children*. Claremont: The Tomás Rivera Center.

Foucault, M. 1977a. *Discipline and Punish: The Birth of the Prison*. Sheridan, A., trans. New York: Pantheon.

Freire, P. 1970. *Pedagogy of the Oppressed*. Rámos, M., trans. New York: Continuum.

———. 1985. *Politics of Education*. South Hadley: Bergin & Garvey.

Freire, P. & Horton, M. 1990. *We Make the Road By Walking: Conversations on Education and Social Change*. Bell, B., Gaventa, J., and Peters, J., eds. Philadelphia: Temple University Press.

Freire, P. & Macedo, D. 1987. *Literacy: Reading the Word and the World*. Massachusetts: Bergin & Garvey.

Freire, P. and Macedo, D. 1998. *Teachers as Cultural Workers: Letters for Those Who Dare Teach*. Boulder: Westview.

Gore, J. M. 1993. *The Struggle for Pedagogies: Critical and Feminist Discourses as Regimes of Truth*. New York: Routledge.

Gramsci. A. 1971. *Selections from the Prison Notebooks*. Medea, Q. and Smith, N., eds. and trans. London: Lawrence & Wishart.

Gutierrez, K. 1991a. "The Effects of Writing Process Instruction on Latino Children." Paper presented at the Annual Meeting of the American Educational Research Association. Chicago, Illinois.

———. 1991b. "Coding Sheet. The Social Contexts of Literacy Study." Kris Gutierrez, principal investigator. An unpublished document. University of California, Los Angeles.

———. 1992. "A Comparison of Instructional Contexts in Writing Process Classrooms with Latino Children." *Education and Urban Society* 24: 244-262.

———. 1993. "Scripts, Counterscripts and Multiple Scripts." Paper presented at the annual meeting of the American Educational Research Association. Atlanta, Georgia.

———. 1994. "How Talk, Context, and Script Shape Contexts for Learning: A Cross-Case Comparison of Journal Sharing." *Linguistics and Education* 5: 335-365.

Gutierrez, K. and Larson, J. 1994. "Language Borders: Recitation as Hegemonic Discourse." *International Journal of Educational Reform* 3: 22-36.

Hughes, L. 1995. Selection from "Song of the Refugee Road." In Rampersad, A. and Roessel, D., eds., *The Collected Poems of Langston Hughes.* New York: Knopf.

Kozol, J. 1985. *Illiterate America.* New York: Plume Press.

Lincoln, Y. and Guba, E. 1985. *Naturalistic Inquiry.* Newbury Park: Sage.

Los Angeles Unified School District. 1990. *The Children Can No Longer Wait! An Action Plan to End Low Achievement and Establish Educational Excellence.* Los Angeles: Los Angeles Unified School District.

McLaren, P. 1989. *Life in Schools: An Introduction to Critical Pedagogy in the Foundations of Education.* New York: Longman.

_____ . 1997. *Revolutionary Multiculturalism: Pedagogies of Dissent for the New Millennium.* Boulder: Westview.

Mehan, H. 1979. *Learning Lessons: Social Organizations in the Classroom.* Cambridge: Harvard University Press.

Miles, M. and Huberman, M. 1984. *Qualitative Data Analysis.* London: Sage.

Oakes, J. Gamoran, A., and Page, R. 1992. "Curriculum Differentiation: Opportunities, Outcomes, and Meaning." In Jackson, P., ed., *Handbook of Research on Curriculum.* New York: MacMillan.

Ochs, E. 1988. *Culture and Language Development.* Cambridge: Cambridge University Press.

O'Hanlon, R. 1988. "Recovering the Subject: Subaltern Studies and Histories of Resistance in Colonial South Asia." *Modern Asian Studies* 22: 222-233.

Pruyn, M. 1994. "Confronting Ignorance and Hate With a Pedagogy of Empowerment: The U.S. 'English Only' Movement and Critical Bilingual Education." *Trans/forms* 1:73-88.

Reading Today. October/November 1993. "U.S. Survey Finds Serious Lack of Literacy Skills." *Reading Today* 11.

Strauss, A. and Corbin, J. 1994. "Grounded Theory Methodology." In Denzin, N. and Lincoln, Y., eds., *Handbook of Qualitative Research.* London: Sage.

Walcott, H. 1988. "Ethnographic Research in Education." In Jaeger, R., ed., *Complimentary Methods for Research in Education.* Washington, D. C.: American Educational Research Association.

Willis, P. 1977. *Learning to Labour.* Lexington: D. C. Heath.

Yin, R. 1984. *Case Study Research.* Beverly Hills: Sage.

Accepting the Word and the World: Accommodating Hegemony

Here, have a dollar
In fact, naw, brotherman, here, have two

—**Arrested Development ("Mr. Wendal")**[1]

In this chapter, the forms of social practice that appeared to inhibit the development of critical student agency in the classroom of Guillermo Linares and his students will be described. Through a presentation and discussion of these findings, it will be shown how the teacher and students co-constructed, through social practices within literacy activities, a "hegemonic discourse community"[2] that seemed to limit the development of critical student agency. The chapter begins with brief representative descriptions of several of Guillermo's students and the physical and pedagogical environment within which they studied in order to contextualize the findings and discussion that comprise the bulk of this chapter.

The Students and The Classroom

During the four months of data collection in Guillermo's classroom, approximately twelve students have been enrolled, although no more than six are present at any given time, due to various work and familial obligations. Four of these students figure prominently in the data because of the representativeness of their contributions during classroom literacy activities. Several of these same students will also become students of Daisy's—their second teacher.

Esteban, a Salvadoran in his late forties, is[3] one of the most academically advanced students in the class. His wife, who has a better command of written Spanish than he does, attends one of *Siempre's* ESL classes.[4] This is the third Spanish literacy program in which Esteban has participated.

Farabundo and Ignacio, who are brothers, are also students in Guillermo's literacy class. Due to a lack of personal transportation, however, they tell me they have difficulty attending classes as regularly as they, and their teacher, would like. Farabundo and Ignacio are also from El Salvador and came to the United States for economic and political reasons seven years ago. Farabundo struggles with written Spanish, but is making slow and steady progress. Ignacio is having more difficulty. As a consequence, Guillermo has put him in "separate instruction." This means, for all intents and purposes, that Ignacio's primary task is to copy syllables and words from a syllable work book (a *silabario*) on his own.

Ana is a grandmother in her early fifties. She is from Nicaragua and came to the United States in the mid-1980s, at the height of the U.S.-backed *Contra* War. I have seen her bring grandchildren to the nearby grade school where I worked for nine years as a school teacher; she also recognizes me. Ana is one of the most advanced students in the class. When I ask her, she says she gained much of her literacy skills during Nicaragua's 1980 Literacy Crusade—see Chapter 2.

Guillermo's intermediate Spanish literacy class shares one large store-front space with the program's beginning Spanish literacy class and an ESL class. No advanced Spanish literacy class currently exists at Siempre. A single steel pillar, painted bright red, serves as the room's only ceiling support. The floor is a dull gray concrete and has many cracks. The plaster walls, while not looking old, do appear as if they have been a bit "roughed up" by the previous tenants. The classes are conducted around six old brown battered office desks that have been arranged in clusters. There are over ninety inexpensive plastic resin chairs stacked up against the walls, but the ESL/literacy project uses fewer than twenty of them. At this point, there are not many students.

Siempre Adelante also uses this store-front for other cultural and political events important to this community. On one door, for example, there is a handwritten sign calling people to a rally at the Guatemalan Consulate to protest the presidential *coup d'état* of several days earlier. There are also frequent fund raisers here for *Siempre* itself as well as for other community-based immigrant support groups. The main entrance is off a parking lot that serves a strip mall. The only other door leading out of this large space faces a dirty sidewalk, and past it, Foxbourne Boulevard, a busy main thoroughfare in the neighborhood. This door is closed and chained, and a security gate is locked before it on the inside. The white walls are bare except for a small electrical box that adorns the West wall. The South wall is decorated with an out-of-date one page calendar featuring a popular Spanish-language singer. There is a small utilitarian bathroom near the main entrance.

Guillermo uses a large chalkboard that has been stood lengthwise on end in one corner of the room. Nadia, the other Spanish literacy teacher, has no chalkboard at all and has her students doing seat work at a large run-down desk with a file cabinet drawer serving as one of its missing legs. The space that houses these three classrooms looks well used and tired. However, it also appears to be in the process of a modest "remodeling" make-over. It is only through a recently successful application for grant funds that these current facilities became available to the education program. By all student, teacher and administrative accounts, this is a step up. The classes used to be held at cramped *Siempre* headquarters and in any other donated neighborhood space made available to them. The main doors are left open, and as the parking lot fills with patrons visiting the neighboring *pupusería*, hair salon and video rental store, a dog barks, bits and pieces of outdoor conversation drift in, distant car alarms wail, children play and birds chirp in the gnarled trees that surround the lot. These are nice sounds, neighborhood sounds. Little yellow flowers that have fallen from the trees form a bright and contrasting blanket on the black asphalt just outside the door.

But people have come here to study. Specifically, Guillermo's students are here to learn how to read and write in Spanish. After they master Spanish literacy, these students would like to go on to learn English in one of the program's three ESL classes. Guillermo begins his course of study by teaching students the names of the letters in the Spanish alphabet and how to print and pronounce them. After this, his goal is to teach the students how to print and pronounce syllabic families comprised of consonant and vowel combinations—for example: *ma, me, mi, mo, mu,* or *pa, pe, pi, po, pu.* As they progress along this phonetic memorization continuum, the students are called upon to decode simple words and short sentences made-up of combinations of one or more of the syllabic families—for example: *"Mi mamá me ama"* ("My mother loves me") or *"Pepe come pupusas"*("Pepe eats *pupusas"*).

"Writing" in this classroom consists almost exclusively of copying letters, syllables and/or words from the blackboard or from *silabarios* at the direction of the teacher. Copying, decoding short de-contextualized passages, and memorizing letter and syllable combinations and sounds is the norm. Overall, there is minimal student-to-student talk and interaction. Class discussions are short in duration and usually involve Guillermo lecturing students about the generative theme of the unit they are studying, with only brief comments and input from students. Instead of resembling what critical pedagogists and educational progressives have detailed as a liberating critical literacy environment (Freire & Macedo 1987; Kozol 1985; Shor & Freire 1987; Weiler 1988), the nature of teaching and learning in this classroom might best be characterized as a "traditional" or "banking" adult literacy setting, just the kind that critical theorists argue against (Freire & Macedo 1987).

Critical Student Agency Postponed:
The Co-Construction of a
Hegemonic Discourse Community

Look like nothing's going to change
Everything still remains the same
I can't do what ten people tell me to do
So I guess I'll remain the same
Just sittin' here restin' my bones
And this loneliness won't leave me alone

—Otis Redding ("Sittin' on the Dock (of the Bay)")[5]

Analysis of the data from literacy activities collected in Guillermo's classroom revealed that a "hegemonic discourse community" was the prevailing form of social practice that was dominant in this classroom, which inhibited the development of critical student agency. Students had been socialized, with some exceptions, to participate in the teacher-centered, hegemonic discourse of the classroom and to conform to hegemonic pedagogical practice at the expense of critical student agency. These practices included acts of student objectification on the part of the teacher and the assumption of conformist stances on the part of the students. It seemed that these student stances were the result of students' and the teacher's socialization to a specific discourse community. The data examples below demonstrate how the students in Guillermo's classroom were discursively positioned by the teacher, and also by themselves, and how through this positioning, a hegemonic discourse community was produced and maintained.

The Discursive Positioning
of Students as "Conformists"
to Hegemonic Pedagogical Practices

On a warm evening in early June, the class was studying a unit whose foci were the Spanish syllables *ga, gue, gui, go, gu,* and the generative word *"guerra"* ("war"). Guillermo begins by talking about war in the Salvadoran context.[6] The predominately Salvadoran students in Guillermo's classroom are intimately familiar with this theme and the reality that Guillermo is describing. While the content of this lesson is socially relevant to the students, I would like to focus on the *nature* of the discourse within which this relevant content is situated because of how that content is positioned and treated within the classroom's discursive practices. The analysis of Example 1[7] will focus on the IRE discourse sequences, how the teacher discursively positions students, and how the students discursively position themselves, in the social practices of this classroom such that the development of critical student agency appears to be hindered. (See "Appendix A" for an explanation of the transcription conventions used in this study.)

Example 1
"War is very heavy for us": Giving the Word and the World

1	Guillermo:	For us, Salvadorans, this word, "war," is very heavy	I I
2		for us. To a Costa Rican, to hear "war" does not cause	
3		any effect. In our country, with 12 years of war, it effects	

4		us. Because of this war, this conflict, this problem, many	
5		of us have had to emigrate. We should know how to	
6		write this word.	

| 7 | Students: | Yes. | R |

| 8 | Guillermo: | It causes, wherever in the world it appears, pain. We | I II |
| 9 | | had more than 70,000 deaths in our country. | |

| 10 | | ((He shows the students a picture of a volcano from an |
| 11 | | FMLN *silabario*[8].)) |

12		A *"Guerrero"* is someone who defends territory, or
13		who makes war. But sometimes the words are used
14		wrong, the state discriminates. For example, the word
15		"terrorist." This is someone who causes terror. This can
16		come from the mountains, or from the barracks. And we
17		know that the FMLN wants to win the peace. Now, we're
18		moving forward. In 1971 and 1972, El Salvador was
19		developing. Then the enemies of progress came in and
20		destroyed our country.

| 21 | Farabundo : | I have a strange question. Who were the enemies who | R |
| 22 | | destroyed our country? |

This classroom interaction, which emerged as representative of the majority of classroom interactions under Guillermo, follows a strict initiation-response discourse pattern and parallels what this study has labeled as a "banking" and hegemonic approach to teaching. Except for IR pair VII (lines 71-77, below), they all follow an IR or IRR pattern. Within this strict IR configuration, there is only room for student responses of one or two words (lines 7, 32, and 48), one sentence (lines 21-22) or gestural responses (lines 31, 47, 50, and 80). Within the social and literate practices of this classroom, brief questions (lines 21-22) or elaborations (lines 33-34 and 69-70) on the part of the students are also acceptable, although not encouraged, by the teacher. Yet we see evidenced a very tightly grounded "recitation script" (Gutierrez 1992, 1994) being employed by Guillermo.

The discourse sequence continues as Guillermo answers Farabundo's question.

23	Guillermo:	From inside and from without.	I III

24		Let's look at the word "communism." It comes from	
25		the word "common," to share things in common. In	
26		this way, Salvadorans should be united. Maybe some	
27		of you suffered during these times, cutting coffee or	
28		something. My brother-in-law was a big owner.	
29		The workers worked and cut all day, and the bosses	
30		rob you.	

| 31 | Students: | [(((Are nodding their heads.)) | R |
| 32 | | [Yes, yes. | |

| 33 | Silvia: | I remember working in coffee and working in cotton. | R |
| 34 | | The bosses always robbed you. | |

| 35 | Guillermo: | There are always those who misinterpret about this. | I IV |

36		The military leaders—I had one in my family, a very	
37		high military official—could do whatever they wanted	
38		economically. They could buy and sell cars. They	
39		didn't pay taxes. And they could cross the borders as	
40		they pleased. But it's not that way anymore. The people	
41		are aware and struggling. There are still some abuses, but	
42		there are less.	

43		Teachers, we can't lie to our students. We have to tell	
44		them the truth. About everything. So the government	
45		labels us "guerrillas." We told the truth. And that truth	
46		hurt the military, the rich.	

| 47 | Students: | [(((Nod their heads.)) | R |
| 48 | | [Yes, yes. | |

Except in one case (line 49), every initiation by Guillermo in this discourse sequence appears to function as a "student objectification"[9] (lines 1, 8, 23, 35, 51, 71, and 78). It seems as if he is attempting to give the students, to "fill them up" with, *one* interpretation of Salvadoran/Central American history. Although the students may be sympathetic with many of Guillermo's viewpoints, he is not giving them an opportunity to demonstrate their agreement or disagreement with him. Instead of leading a discussion on war and the politics of Central America and Caribbean—on issues such as the Salvadoran war and government, land owners and bosses, military leaders, political killings, the FMLN, communism, the role of teachers in "enlightening" students or the politics of Cuba—Guillermo is giving the students *his* interpretation of these issues. This in-and-of-itself is not student objectification, but when combined with the observation that Guillermo is in strict control of classroom talk—through tight IR/IRE patterns, and the fact that students are not given many opportunities to bid for the floor or talk—students do become objectified through the way the teacher is using discourse. Not inviting or allowing students to share extended elaborations of their views on his lecture topics has the effect of positioning students as passive social subjects who are to absorb the "facts" that are given to them.

The one exception is Guillermo's initiation on line 49 ("So they killed thousands of teachers. Remember?"). This initiation was coded as a weak "student *subjectification*."[10] In this instance Guillermo does ask the students a question, and therefore invites them to participate in the discussion. They do so by nodding their heads.

49 Guillermo: So they killed thousands of teachers. Remember?   I V

50 Students: ((Nod their heads.))   R

51 Guillermo: Because we opened the eyes of the students.   I VI

52   ((He relates a story about teaching his students in El
53   Salvador the difference between a "republic" and a
54   "dictatorship," labeling the government of El Salvador
55   a "dictatorship."))

56   This is what I told my students. But the problem was
57   that we had intercoms in our classrooms. And the
58   principal of the school had been listening in on what I
59   had been teaching. She called me in to her office right
60   away. She told me that what I was saying was
61   "inappropriate." And I told her that she ought to get
62   a dictionary and look-up the word 'dictatorship'
63   herself.

64   It's important for you to know this, often we criticize
65   without knowing. So we should know the word
66   "guerra" and the syllable "gue." Monday, we'll write

| 67 | | this word, and this syllable, and we'll make a |
| 68 | | paragraph. |

| 69 | A student: | Once the army came and took over our school in | R |
| 70 | | El Salvador. They accused us of being "Cubans." |

In their responses to Guillermo's initiations in this representative discourse sequence, students frequently assumed "conformist stances."[11] Eight of the eleven responses made by students during this discourse sequence conformed to hegemonic pedagogical practice. Five of these eight responses were coded as "conformist stances," where students either responded by nodding their heads in agreement (line 50), nodding their heads in agreement and answering "yes" (lines 31-32, 47-48) or silently obeying the teacher's directives (line 80). Three out of these eight responses, while not being coded as outright conformist stances, were conformist in nature. They involved asking a question (lines 21-22: "Who were the enemies who destroyed our country?") and offering two short student elaborations of the themes that were the focus of Guillermo's lecture (lines 33-34: "I remember working in coffee and working in cotton. The bosses always robbed you"; and lines 69-70: "Once the army came and took over our school in El Salvador. They accused us of being 'Cubans'"). While not coded as conformist stances, these responses were conformist in nature in that they did not go against the apparent hegemonic social practices of this classroom.

Additionally, there is very little "up-take" of student questions in Guillermo's initiations. It does occur on three occasions: in line 23 ("From inside and from without"), in line 35 ("There are always those who misinterpret about this") and in line 71 ("Cuba is a free country"). However, the teacher's up-takes manifest as very brief comments or answers, and then he continues forward with his monologue without incorporating the content of the student question or elaboration. The discursive practices documented here were representative of the social practices this class regularly engaged in during literacy activities.

The three remaining student responses were coded as student "resistant stances,"[12] for in these instances, the students strongly (if only briefly) diverged from the hegemonic practices of the classroom. These resistant stances all occurred during one interaction, which begins with Guillermo addressing a student's elaboration (see directly above, lines 69-70), as follows:

71	Guillermo:	Cuba is a free country.	I VII
72		((Elaborates his supportive thoughts on Cuba.))	
73	Students:	((Begins to discuss their divergent thoughts on Cuba.))	R
74	Farabundo:	((To Guillermo:))	
75		Then why do so many Cubans come to this country?	R
76		Cuba is a big country.	
77	Students:	[((Begin to talk about Cuba and the former Soviet Union.))	R

During this interaction students begin to take resistant stances in line 73, in response to Guillermo's opinions on Cuba. A clear resistant stance is taken by Farabundo in lines 75-76, when he offers a direct *challenge* to Guillermo's position ("Then why do so many Cubans come to this country? Cuba is a big country"). This response might alternatively be coded as an "agentive stance," in that Farabundo might be attempting to alter the hegemonic pedagogical order, to force Guillermo to break with the recitation script and enter into more of a discussion, or debate, with the students on some of the issues he has raised. But this goes to Farabundo's intentionality. Is he intentionally trying to change the discourse of the classroom from hegemonic to counter-hegemonic? Or is he simply trying to be obstinate or "difficult" as a way of resisting the prevailing order, of showing discontent? These questions cannot be answered from the data, so this student response was left as "resistant." This does not diminish the fact, however, that this move on Farabundo's part is significant. It is a direct challenge to Guillermo's authority. The discourse sequence, and the students' responses, continues in line 71, with the students beginning to expand their conversation on Cuba to include the former Soviet Union.

As this resistant sequence unfolds through these three student responses, the adult learners begin to articulate views different from those of their teacher. But Guillermo stops this.

| 78 | Guillermo: | [We can continue this discussion on Monday. It's late, | I VIII |
| 79 | | and class is over for the evening. | |

| 80 | Students: | ((Pack up and leave.)) | R |

Just as the students begin to expand their discussion to include the former Soviet Union, Guillermo ends the interaction. Based on the program's stated objectives, this literacy activity, as well as *all* literacy and pedagogical activities in the classrooms—which focused on the generative theme of "war" in El Salvador—was to have included the bringing in of examples from the students' real life experiences[13] as Salvadorans. But it was the teacher who dominated the discourse and elaborated these experiences *for* the students. As students' responses supported the teacher's instantiation of this activity, their in-put was accommodated—although not necessarily invited. But as the students' began to resist these practices (as they began to do in line 73), the activity was stopped by Guillermo. He tells students to go home (lines 78-79), and they comply without further comment (line 80). Cuba is not brought up as a discussion topic during the next class meeting.

In the above literacy activity, a strict IR discourse pattern and teacher recitation script are being used. Further, Guillermo is "objectifying" his students by *giving* them the sociopolitical content for the generative theme of "war," as opposed to co-constructing it with them through dialogue, as the teachers had been trained to do. Additionally, students themselves are contributing to the hegemonic social practices exhibited during this activity by assuming "conformist stances." By not resisting or challenging the way Guillermo is running this activity, the students are in essence acquiescing to and validating Guillermo's approach. When they do begin to resist the teacher, through opposition to his interpretation of Cuban politics, they are shut down. These social practices on the part of the teacher, and his students, combined to reinforce a hegemonic understanding of the learning process; an understanding where students are seen as "empty" and agency is discouraged.

In Example 2, below, Guillermo gives a dictation to his students. It is Guillermo's expectation that all will participate. This does not happen. This example will continue to examine how students were discursively situated by themselves, and by their teacher, in the social practices of this classroom—as will all of the following examples in this and in Chapters 5 and 6—and what that portended for the development of critical student agency.

Example 2
Resisting the Dictation

1	Guillermo:	Now I'll dictate to you. Write "dictation."	I
2		((He dictates the following:))	
3		"*En otoño sopla el viento y los árboles en la plaza*	
4		*se quedan sin hojas.*"	
5		"In autumn, the wind blows and the trees in the plaza	
6		are left without leaves."	
7	Ana:	((Writes:))	R
8		*En otoño sopla el viento y los árboles*	
9		*en la plaza, se quedan sin hojas.*	
10		"In autumn, the wind blows and the trees	
11		in the plaza are left without leaves."	
12	Farabundo:	((Begins writing down what Guillermo has dictated,	R
13		appears to become frustrated, stops, and starts	
14		sharpening his pencil intently, never getting back	
15		to the assignment.))	
16	Benita/ Ignacio:	((Continue with their individual assignments, and do	R
17		not participate in the dictation.))	

In response to Guillermo's initiation (line 1), Ana conforms and writes down what he dictates to the class in her notebook (lines 7-11). Farabundo (line 12) begins by conforming, becomes frustrated, and starts to resist (line 13), performing an activity at which he will have more success: sharpening his pencil. He never returns to the dictation. Benita and Ignacio, the other two students present on this day, are also expected to write down Guillermo's dictation, even though they have been given "separate instruction," due to their "low" ability levels. Instead of complying, they resist (lines 16-17),[14] and continue copying from their *silabarios*, in direct defiance of Guillermo's instructions. He says nothing.

Example 3
"Some students are not serious":
Passive Resistance and Subtle "Discipline"

On this evening, the class was completing a literacy activity that included copying from the board. Farabundo finishes before the rest of the class and begins to pack up and leave for the evening, despite the fact that Guillermo has not yet dismissed the class, as was his practice.

1	Farabundo:	((Leaves early, at 8:55.))	
2	Guillermo:	Can I make you some homework?	I
3	Farabundo:	No.	R
4 5	Ignacio:	((Packs his things, and silently follows his brother Farabundo. Does not ask for homework.))	
6 7	Guillermo:	((To Ana, Benita—the remaining students —and myself:))	E
8 9 10		Some students are not serious. They don't want to do homework. They think I'm mean, too demanding. They eventually leave the class.	

After Farabundo gets up and leaves early (line 1), Guillermo initiates an interaction by asking Farabundo if he can prepare a homework for him (line 2). Homework preparation consists of the teacher writing a list of syllables or words across the top of a blank piece of paper, which the student is then to copy down to the bottom. In his response (line 3), Farabundo assumes a resistant stance, and declines the offer. Ignacio then leaves right after his brother without a word to the teacher (lines 4-5), also assuming a resistant stance. Guillermo does not address or discipline Ignacio as he leaves. After he is gone, however, the teacher disciplines (and "evaluates") both Farabundo and Ignacio in absentia. He turns and says to me and the two remaining students, "Some students are not serious. They don't want to do homework. They think I'm mean, too demanding. They eventually leave the class" (lines 6-10). This also serves as a subtle warning to Ana and Benita that conformism is preferred to resistance. Earlier, during the same evening's instruction, Ana assumed a conformist stance as she wrote down Guillermo's dictation (Example 2, lines 6-7), while Benita (along with Ignacio, and eventually Farabundo) assumed resistant stances by not doing the same assignment (Example 2, lines 16-17).

Resistant stances seem to be most successful in this classroom when they assume the form of passive non-compliance. Passive resistant stances are evidenced in Example 2 by Farabundo (lines 13-15), and Benita and Ignacio (lines 16-17), and in Example 3 by Farabundo (line 3) and Ignacio (lines 4-5). Additionally, Ignacio frequently assumes passive resistant stances by ignoring Guillermo's requests that he read or copy syllables or words from the board. Instead, he often turns to me and—in hushed and conspiratorial tones—begins reading words he *knows* how to read from his *silabario*. At times, these types of passive resistance do serve to get students out of performing certain tasks in this classroom. Despite these occasional resistant student stances, however, Guillermo's hegemonic pedagogical practices appear to continue unabated until he eventually quits the program, and another teacher takes over in his stead. Throughout his tenure at *Siempre*, Guillermo never changes his practices of discouraging dialogue or discussion among students by dominating most classroom talk or of lecturing *to* students about a particular "generative theme" (telling them what they need to know and how they need to know it). Finally, my coding and analysis of the literacy activities under Guillermo revealed a consistent use, on his part, of a strict IR discourse pattern (as in Example 1) and a "recitation script."

While Guillermo had adopted some of the semantic surface trappings of the Freirean approach his actual discursive implementation of this pedagogy appeared far from Freirean. To fully implement the Freirean/critical approach might prove too much of a strain on the teacher-centered, "banking" pedagogical belief system he had reported being socialized to as both a student and a teacher. This would have involved extensive dialogue, discussion, disagreement and more symmetrical power relations between him and his students. Guillermo seemed only able to implement a traditional hegemonic pedagogy with a veneer of Freireanism. An example of his reluctance to fully engage the Freirean process, with specific regard to elaborated dialogue and discussion with students, became evident during a teacher training session in early August of 1993. Guillermo and Daisy, the coordinator of Siempre's ESL and Spanish literacy project, and the person who would soon replace Guillermo as teacher in his classroom, were planing a literacy unit around the generative theme of "housing." Daisy had been brainstorming possible sub-topics that could be brought up in classroom discussion based on students' experiences. Guillermo was concerned that bringing up these topics would be unwieldy, and too much for the students to be able to handle. The following example from Daisy and Guillermo's conversation demonstrates how Guillermo is ill-at-ease with allowing students too much freedom in classroom activities.

Example 4
"That's a lot to talk about."

Guillermo: There's lots to talk about, to discuss, with this theme. Sometimes, there are some things they can't write, can't do. It's too much.

Daisy: Yes they can. I'd like you to let them try. If they are capable of profoundly analyzing a theme, they're capable of dealing with the language. Let them.

     The history of the area, the big houses, the wealthy who left, how the homes are now sub-divided, not maintained.

Guillermo: That's a lot to talk about.

Through this dialogue with Daisy, we see how Guillermo is reluctant to engage students beyond the level of listening and copying. It would be, in Guillermo's words, "too much" for them to handle. But the data seem to indicate that it might actually be too much for *Guillermo* to handle (see Example 1, lines 78-79, above).

Lessons Learned: Self-Imposed Conformism and The Maintenance of Hegemony

One evening, when Guillermo had stepped away from his students for a few minutes, I asked them, "What do you prefer, copying sentences like these from the board, or making up your own?" I asked this question because this was the task in which they were most often engaged. They all agreed that they preferred to copy sentences from the board that Guillermo had selected and written. Pedro looked at me and said, in a matter-of-fact and resigned voice, *"De nosotros sale nada"* ("From us comes nothing.") It seems that the hegemonic social practices they co-constructed with Guillermo in the classroom—along with their previous exposures to "banking" pedagogy[15]—had indeed "taught" them that they should not view themselves as more than passive social subjects acted upon by others. They had learned this lesson despite their occasional, yet noteworthy, acts of resistance within the classroom. They were discursively self-disciplining themselves so efficiently that even Michel would blush. When Guillermo was not present to enforce it, they bought into the prevailing hegemony and defined themselves as empty. Not only did these students place themselves *low* on the knowledge hierarchy, but, as one might expect, they placed their teacher very *high* on it. The extended excerpt from field notes, presented below in Example 5, shows just how high.

Example 5
Day of the "Apostle"

1 Toward the end of this day's thirty minutes of instruction—the classes
2 normally last two hours—many people, including the students who meet in
3 the other storefront, begin to fill the large common room. Lots of good smelling,
4 homemade dishes covered with tinfoil and wrapped in plastic bags, and
5 bottles of orange, brown and light green soda, start to fill two tables that
6 have been pushed together at the front of the room. The students' families and
7 friends have also come tonight. There are many new faces. As it turns out, the
8 Salvadoran "Day of the Teacher" was yesterday. So this evening, a collective
9 party for all five classes is planned instead of holding regular meetings, in
10 honor of the program's teachers: Guillermo, Nadia, Oscar, Rubén and
11 Cristina. This is an unexpected surprise for the teachers. They didn't know
12 that their students had been planning this for them. There are approximately
13 50-60 people in attendance. The teachers and the program coordinator are
14 asked to sit in front of the assembled group, overlooking the food, in a place
15 of honor. At the insistence of the student organizers, and over my protests, I
16 am also asked to sit with the other teachers up in front, even though I am not a
17 teacher for *Siempre Adelante*. They say, "That doesn't matter, you are a
18 teacher." (They know I work down the street at the neighborhood school.) I
19 join the others. Rosa, a heavyset woman in her late 50s from Rubén's ESL
20 class, who is known as an activist among her classmates, shares her thoughts
21 and gives a "testimonial" on this Day of the Teacher. She says she has known

22 Guillermo for 10 years, ever since he taught her daughter back in El Salvador
23 at his school, before they all came into exile here in the United States. She
24 praises her teacher Rubén, Guillermo, the other teachers with the program,
25 and Daisy, the program coordinator. She says she has learned much from her
26 teacher, has much respect for teachers in general, and for all the important
27 work that they do. She refers to teachers as "apostles of literacy," and
28 "warriors against ignorance." The assembled crowd of now 80 people
29 vocalizes its agreement. There are several other student "testimonials"—by
30 the other event organizers, and by whomever is moved to speak from the
31 audience. The teachers are then given wrapped presents. As they open them,
32 the crowd of students and well-wishers is excited for and with them. The
33 party continues with plates of food being given to each teacher (including
34 myself), and then to the rest of the crowd. Later, after the food, there is music
35 and dancing.

Through this interaction, the students demonstrate in what high regard they hold their teachers by organizing the celebration itself; by placing the teachers in front of the assembly (lines 13-15); by offering "testimonials" in their honor (lines 20-31); by presenting them with gifts (line 31); and by serving them food before everyone else (lines 32-34). But possibly even more dramatically, Rosa (lines 27-28) describes teachers as *apostles* ("of literacy") and *warriors* ("against ignorance"), and the assembled group of eighty students and supporters concurs. When one's teacher takes on biblical proportions, conforming to her or his classroom practice is a much easier than resisting or attempting to change it. At this point, to paraphrase Foucault (1977:203), exterior power has given way to an internal, productive power. The students have become hegemonized.

Finally, excerpts from an interview conducted with Guillermo's students after he quit the program will be presented. In their answers to my questions, it becomes clear how entrenched the students themselves have become in the hegemonic practices of the classroom, even when they no longer have Guillermo as a teacher.

Example 6
"Through dictation and memorizing words": An Interview with Students

1 Marc: How do adults best learn to read and write?

2 Juan: It has to do with the attitude of the student, if they pay
3   attention. And also the intelligence of the teacher.

4	Samuel:	By reviewing a board full of words.
5	Veronica:	Through dictation and memorizing words.
6	Esteban:	Letters. Syllables.
7 8	Gloria:	The Sir puts words on the board, explains how to read them, and reviews them.
9 10	Marc:	What is the role of the teacher, and of the student, in this process?
11 12	Juan:	The teacher has to say what is right and what is wrong. The student has to pay attention.
13	Marc:	Have you improved your literacy? Are you making progress?
14	Veronica:	You have to have a lot of persistence. I say it's good.
15	Juan:	The teacher knows what one can do.
16 17	Esteban:	I was seeing in Mr. Linares that we weren't advancing quickly, or well.
18	Veronica:	No. He said that it was a problem of people not coming.

During this interview, the students were very candid with their responses. It seemed that they had become as comfortable with me as I had with them. I had come to their class every Thursday evening for two hours over the past several months. I was an outsider, but one who grew to be trusted. I had worked as their "substitute" on two occasions when Guillermo had been absent, and they occasionally turned to me for advice on their assignments during class. We had come to know quite a bit about one another. So it came as no surprise when they shared openly with me their views on the process of literacy development, the appropriate roles of teachers and students, and if they thought they were advancing within this process. By and large, they all saw the literacy process as mechanistic. Learning to read and write involved reviewing words on the board, dictation, memorization and studying letters and syllables (lines 2-6). Gloria put it even more directly (lines 7-8): "The Sir puts words on the board, explains how to read them, and reviews them."

On "appropriate" teacher and student roles, the group was also in consensus. The teacher determines right or wrong (line 11) and "knows what one can do" (line 15). The student's role was to "pay attention" (line 12) and to be persistent (line 14). Even with this general agreement regarding the existing order, however, there was some displeasure and resistance voiced when Esteban (lines 16-17) says, "I was seeing in Mr. Linares that we weren't advancing quickly. Or well." Although this comment is quickly countered by Veronica's conformist statement (line 18): "No. He said that it was a problem of people not coming," Esteban's comments point out a chink in the armor of this classroom's hegemonic practices, for Esteban is noting that there was something wrong with the instruction they had received under Guillermo.

Esteban's comments notwithstanding, the overriding opinions of this group were in support of the hegemonic pedagogical practices they had come to know under Guillermo. In a sense, maybe they had to support these practices, for they participated in their creation and maintenance along with the teacher. And just because Guillermo had left, they were not now going to automatically change this internalized cultural/pedagogical logic of the classroom—even if they at times resisted it.

While these forms of social interaction appeared to limit the development of student agency, this did not happen in a vacuum. The teacher and the students co-constructed a shared understanding of what constituted legitimate and appropriate interaction in their classroom. They developed a social and cultural understanding of literacy instruction as a solitary, repetitious act where information and knowledge flowed from the teacher to the students. Both the students and the teacher would frequently describe this process of literacy instruction and acquisition as "tedious," "difficult" and "boring." The students would agree that even though learning to read and write was difficult and unenjoyable, this was just the way one learns. Guillermo and his students created this social and cultural definition of teaching and learning together.

Understanding Guillermo's Classroom

The discursive practices of Guillermo and his students, as operationalized in the representative literacy activities presented above

(Examples 1 through 3), show how Guillermo consistently positioned students as passive subjects through student objectification. These examples also show how Guillermo's students self-positioned as passive social subjects through conformist stances—with some notable exceptions where they assume resistant stances (with mixed results). Through these social practices, this group of students was accommodating the hegemonic pedagogical order and accepting the "word" *and* the "world" of the teacher. And this had one major result: there was an almost total lack of observed critical student agency development among the students during the four months of data collection in Guillermo's classroom. Farabundo's comment during the "Cuba incident" from Example 1 above (lines 75-76) is the only time a student's response came *close* to being coded as an agentive stance.

Guillermo and his students created a discourse community that produced and maintained the hegemonic pedagogical order; an order that saw students as passive objects whose lot it was to accept the "word" and the "world" of the teacher, and to obediently absorb the discrete facts the teacher gave them. Within this pedagogical vision in Guillermo's classroom, my analysis of the data revealed that there was little room for the emergence of critical student agency. And indeed, little critical student agency developed, despite the fact that the classroom was situated within a larger Freirean-inspired program *whose specific goal* it was to foster critical consciousness and critical student agency among its learners.

What emerged from the data were two patterns of behavior: one where the teacher, Guillermo, consistently positioned his students as passive social subjects through the discourse of the classroom; and another where his students similarly positioned themselves, a majority of the time, as passive social subjects through assuming conformist stances within classroom discourse. Although there were notable exceptions where the students assumed resistant stances, for the most part, they conformed to Guillermo and the hegemonic pedagogical practices he embraced. In this classroom, the teacher and the students co-constructed a shared understanding of what constituted legitimate and appropriate interaction in their classroom: one that excluded students from assuming roles as pedagogical or sociopolitical change agents. While

Guillermo used some of the language of the Freirean approach, his actual discursive implementation of this pedagogy was far from Freirean. Rather, he continued to manifest a teacher-centered, "banking" pedagogical belief system in the classroom.

Thus, as the data illustrate, hegemonic pedagogical practice was the form of social practice that was dominant in the classroom of Guillermo Linares and his students, and this limited the development of critical student agency. This pedagogical practice was discursively constructed and maintained over time, even after Guillermo and his students were separated.

In the next chapter, "Reading the Word through the World: Constructing a Counter-Hegemony," we will shift gears and visit the classroom of Daisy Contreras and *her* students—for the most part, the same students that studied under Guillermo—and describe the kinds, and nature, of social and discursive interactions in which they engaged, and what this meant for the development of critical student agency.

Notes

1. Words and music by Todd Thomas. (c) Copyright 1992 EMI BLACKWOOD MUSIC. INC. and ARRESTED DEVELOPMENT MUSIC. All Rights on behalf of ARRESTED DEVELOPMENT MUSIC Controlled and Administered by EMI BLACKWOOD MUSIC INC. All Rights Reserved. International Copyright Secured. Used by Permission. *Reprinted by Permission of Hal Leonard Corporation.*

2. In this study, I use the term, "hegemonic discourse community," to refer to a community of learners whose "Discourse" supports hegemonic pedagogical practices. By "Discourse," as noted earlier, I mean teacher's and students' ways of speaking, writing, behaving, thinking, valuing, interacting and feeling (Gee 1990).

3. In this and the following two chapters, I will use the present tense as I describe the students, the teachers, the physical classroom environments within which they worked, and as I share and analyze the representative data samples they all produced. While this study and the observations that inform it is about a snap-shot in time (in the *past*), I want the reader to be able to experience the same sense of immediacy, urgency and intimacy that hung in the air, and that I felt as a researcher, in this fascinating and instructive pedagogical setting.

4. In order to be matriculated into one of *Siempre's* ESL classes, prospective students first have to demonstrate proficiency in written Span-

ish.

5. *(Sittin' On) THE DOCK OF THE BAY,* by Otis Redding and Stephen Cropper. (c) 1968/1975 East/Memphis Music Corp. (c) (Renewed), Assigned to Irving Music, Inc. All Rights Reserved. Used by Permission. WARNER BROS. PUBLICATIONS U.S. INC., Miami, FL 33014.

6. There was open warfare between a succession of U.S.-supported right-wing dictatorships and a leftist *guerrilla* movement (the FMLN) from the late 1970s through 1991, when a peace accord was signed between the parties. Although a tense peace has been in place since that time, human rights abuses, "disappearances" and "death squad" (i.e., U.S.-backed Salvadoran secrete police) activities continue.

7. The initiation-response sequences of Example 1 are drawn from one discourse sequence of a literacy activity. These IR sequences, denoted by Roman numerals in the upper right-hand corner of each segment, are broken-up here for ease of analysis and discussion. To view the complete and uninterrupted discourse sequence, see "Appendix B." All other subsequent data examples, except for Example 4, can also be found, sequentially, in the APPENDICES.

8. During the war in El Salvador, the Salvadoran government—and their U.S. advisors and benefactors—were never able to fully rout the FMLN rebels from their volcanic mountain stronghold near the capital. It was common knowledge among the populace that the *guerrilla* had their headquarters at this location. So for this group of Salvadoran students in Los Angeles, there was an immediate connection between this drawing of a volcano, and the FMLN—as was probably the intention of those who produced the *silabario*.

9. An act of "student objectification" occurs when the teacher attempts to discursively position students as objects of instruction, as passive social subjects. This follows a hegemonic/banking/recitation pedagogical model of teaching, where students are understood as the one-way receivers of teachers' knowledge.

10. An act of "student subjectification" occurs when the teacher attempts to discursively position students as active social subjects. This follows a counter-hegemonic pedagogical model of teaching where students co-construct classroom knowledge with the teacher and their classmates.

11. A "conformist stance" is assumed by students when they discursively position themselves as passive social subjects ("objects") to be acted upon by the teacher. The student complies with the directives and mandates of the teacher and offers no observable resistance or opposition to hegemonic pedagogical practices.

12. A "resistant stance" is assumed when a student discursively po-

sitions herself or himself in *opposition* to classroom hegemonic social practices. While being discursively positioned as a "passive social subject" or even an "object" by the teacher, this student attempts to *resist* objectification. This resistance often takes the form of purposefully ignoring or disobeying a teacher who is following a "banking" (Freire 1970) or "recitation" (Gutierrez 1992) pedagogical model or script. While resistance is offered, a preferable set of counter-hegemonic pedagogical practices are not usually advanced.

13. As elaborated during teacher training sessions that were held by *Siempre* to familiarize their teachers with the Freirean approach.

14. This was coded as resistant because Farabundo, Benita and Ignacio have all demonstrated the ability to take dictation in the past. In this instance, they choose not to.

15. Recall from Chapter 3 that all students who had had previous schooling experiences reported studying in teacher-centered classrooms similar to Guillermo's.

References

Foucault, M. 1977. *Discipline and Punish: The Birth of the Prison.* Sheridan, A., trans. New York: Pantheon.

Freire, P. & Macedo, D. 1987. *Literacy: Reading the Word and the World.* Massachusetts: Bergin & Garvey.

Gee, J. 1990. *Social Linguistics and Literacies: Ideology and Discourses.* London: Falmer.

Gutierrez, K. 1992. "A Comparison of Instructional Contexts in Writing Process Classrooms with Latino Children." *Education and Urban Society* 24: 244-262.

_____. 1994. "How Talk, Context, and Script Shape Contexts for Learning: A Cross-Case Comparison of Journal Sharing." *Linguistics and Education* 5: 335-365.

Kozol, J. 1985. *Illiterate America.* New York: Plume Press.

Shor, I. and Freire, P. 1987. *A Pedagogy for Liberation: Dialogues on Transforming Education.* Massachusetts: Bergin & Garvey.

Weiler, K. 1988. *Women Teaching for Change: Gender, Class and Power.* South Hadley: Bergin & Garvey.

5

Reading the Word through the World: Constructing a Counter-Hegemony

Organizing the people is the process which the revolutionary leaders, who are also prevented from saying their own word, initiate the experience of learning how to name the world...[L]eaders cannot say their word alone: they must say it with the people.

—Paulo Freire (1970:179)

In this chapter, the findings on the forms of social practice that appeared to foster the development of critical student agency in the classroom of Daisy Contreras and her students will be presented. The data will show that a "counter-hegemonic discourse community" was modeled by Daisy and then slowly co-constructed by her and her students, and that this discourse community challenged hegemonic pedagogical practices and eventually lead to the development of critical student agency. The chapter will begin with brief descriptions of Daisy, several of her students, and the physical and pedagogical environment in which they worked in order to contextualize the subsequently presented findings and discussion.

The Students and The Classroom

Esteban, Farabundo and Ignacio continue as students under Daisy. Gloria, who began to study with Guillermo during the last month of his tenure at *Siempre Adelante*, also continues under Daisy. According to Daisy's assessment, Gloria, a Salvadoran woman in her early twenties, has low to intermediate literacy skills. She is out-going, friendly and works at a camper shell assembly plant. Gloria periodically complains that her hands are sore from handling the sharp edges of the plastic windows it is her job to install in the shells. Veronica, Juan and Samuel, all new students, join the class.

Veronica, who has been assessed by the teacher as one of the most academically advanced students, is a quiet and very serious woman in her mid-thirties. Juan is a mechanic and has a wife and two sons who occasionally join him in class. And he is politically active in several Central American organizations in the city. Samuel, a young Salvadoran man in his twenties, is energetic, speaks with a slight speech impediment and attends class only occasionally. Ana, the grandmother from Nicaragua who studied under Guillermo, as well as several other students, attend class less and less frequently, and eventually stop coming altogether. Overall, there are approximately six students who regularly come to class. The actual enrollment remains at approximately twelve.

The physical site where the Spanish literacy classes are held has undergone a transformation during the winter break. The once large store-front has been sub-divided by removable walls. Instead of a single large space being shared by several classes, there are now individual rooms where classes are held separately. While the classes can still hear each other working and talking (the walls do not continue all the way up to the ceiling), the environment is much more conducive to small group interaction and concentration. There are many more students since I began collecting data in June. Where there were approximately forty-five students in five classes at the beginning, there are now approximately one hundred ten students in seven classes. The Spanish literacy classes have remained at two, but their internal numbers have increased—although not all students attend class every day. And the ESL classes have also increased in both number (there are more ESL classes) and size (there are more students per class). This has been due to a vigorous community-wide information and student recruitment campaign by *Siempre*. Additionally, a Student Council has been elected and makes regular decisions about issues facing the program and students, including program fund raising, improvements and changes in the program itself, and how to most efficiently allocate the program's scarce resources. Through fund-raising activities organized by the Council—such as parties, dances and food sales—pedagogical materials including dictionaries, a television and video cassette recorder, and tape recorders have been purchased and are now used regularly in all of the classes. Additionally, each classroom now has its own chalk or white erase board. There have been many improvements.

Walking into Daisy's classroom and looking at what is on the chalkboard and walls, it is difficult to notice, at first, a significant difference between her and Guillermo's classrooms. There are still the familiar lists of syllabic families (*ma, me, mi, mo, mu; ra, re, ri, ro, ru; da, de, di, do, du;* and *sa, se, si, so , su*), lists of words drawn from those syllables and short texts on the board and walls. But, upon further inspection, a difference is noted. After questioning the teacher and class members, one learns that most of these words and texts have been produced by the students and not the teacher. Further, most of the themes from which these syllables, words and short texts were drawn were generated by the students and teacher together. Additionally, the content of classroom writing has shifted. Instead of words like *mamá, regalo, dedo* and *seco* ("mother," "present," "finger" and "dry"), one is now more likely to see words like *renta, drogas, sindicato, dueño, SIDA* and *inmigración* ("rent," "drugs," "trade union," "boss," "AIDS" and "immigration."). Instead of sentences like *"Mi mamá me ama,"* ("Mother loves me"), one is more likely to find sentences like *"Los dueños abusan los derechos de los inmigrantes"* ("Bosses abuse the rights of immigrants").[1] And finally, one finds that texts are more likely to have come from students and be grounded in classroom discussions of political issues, rather than from the teacher or textbooks—whether these are textbooks on "official" Spanish grammar from Spain or *silabarios* produced by the FMLN (see Example 7, below).

In Daisy's classroom, one gets the sense that she is seen as an "authority" by her students, but not as "authoritarian" (to draw Freire's distinction). They turn to her for the "right" answers, and for correction, but there is a feeling in the classroom that the teacher and students are on the same side of the table. It is as if they are struggling *together* to help students gain mastery of written Spanish; instead of at opposite sides with the teacher possessing a single "knowledge" and "truth" that is to be dispensed to them, and the students being "ignorant" and "empty." There is more of a feeling of *"De ellos, sí sale algo,"* ("From them, something *does* come" as opposed to *"De ellos, no sale nada"* ("From them, comes nothing"). I believe these ethnographic "feelings" and "senses" will be borne-out in the data and discussion that follow.

The Gradual Emergence of Agency
Through the Co-Construction of
a Counter-Hegemonic Discourse Community

Analysis of the data from the literacy activities collected in Daisy's classroom revealed that a "counter-hegemonic pedagogy" was the prevailing form of social practice that slowly became dominant in this classroom. This form of social practice appeared to foster the development of critical student agency. Students had been *re*-socialized, with some exceptions, to participate in a more student-centered, egalitarian form of discourse in this classroom. Consequently, forms of student resistance and agency to traditional hegemonic pedagogical practices—as they had experienced under Guillermo and with most previous teachers—appeared to increase. The data examples below will demonstrate how the students in Daisy's classroom were discursively positioned by the teacher, and by themselves, such that this counter-hegemonic discourse community was produced. These data examples are representative of a pattern of student "subjectification" on the part of the teacher, and student "resistant" and "agentive" stances on the part of the students. This pattern emerged from an analysis of the class' social practices within literacy activities.

The Discursive Positioning of Students as Agents Against Hegemonic Social Practices

Example 7
War, Part II

In this discourse sequence, Daisy and her students are studying the syllables *ga, gue, gui, go, gu,* and the generative word *"guerra"*(war)—much as Guillermo had done with many of these same students five months earlier. This lesson will involve a discussion of the war in El Salvador and the generation of a text from that discussion. To begin, Daisy suggests that they put a sentence on the board dealing with war. Esteban comes up with, *"La guerra no es buena*" ("War is not good," or "The war is not good"). Daisy writes this on the board, and then asks her students the following question.

1	Daisy:	Using your ideas, how could we extend this sentence?	I I
2	Farabundo:	*La guerra no es buena porque*	R
3		*ha destruido mucho el país.*	
4		War is bad because it has	
5		destroyed the country much.	
6	Daisy:	((Changes the sentence to read:))	
7		*La guerra no es buena porque*	R
8		*ha destruido mucho el país.*	
9		War is bad because it has	
10		destroyed the country much.	
11		This sentence tells me much more.	E
12	Gloria:	Let's put "El Salvador."	R
13	Daisy:	Where should I put it?	I II
14	Farabundo:	*"La guerra de El Salvador no es buena porque*	R
15		*ha destruido mucho el país,"* o	
16		*"La guerra no es buena porque*	
17		*ha destruido mucho el país de El Salvador."*	
18		"The war of *EL Salvador* is not good	
19		because it has destroyed the country much," or	
20		"The war is not good because it has	
21		destroyed the country of El Salvador much."	
22	Daisy:	((Changes the sentence to read:))	R
23		*La guerra de El Salvador no es buena porque*	
24		*ha destruido mucho el país.*	
25		The war of EL Salvador is not good	
26		because it has destroyed the country much.	
27		*La guerra de El Salvador no es buena porque*	R
28		*ha destruido mucho el país.*	
29		The war of EL Salvador is not good because	
30		it has destroyed the country much.	

In beginning to analyze this discourse sequence, we see that Daisy and her students are using a very relaxed interpretation of the IRE model. As we consider the IRRER and IRRR patterns that begin this discourse sequence (I and II, above), and especially the IRRERRRRRER pattern with which it ends (III, below), it appears that the students and the teacher are indeed building on "one another's responses in a manner that more closely resembles a conversational discourse structure" (Gutierrez 1991a:7). We can see, for example, how more turn-taking is involved in this discourse sequence. It is also evident that the students and teacher all have numerous opportunities to speak, as compared to typical discourse patterns that emerged under Guillermo. Discursive interactions involving IRE patterns such as these, in combination with other contextual variations, have been described by Gutierrez (1991b) as indicating the presence of a "responsive"—as opposed to "recitation"—teaching script. And responsive teaching scripts indicate that the social practices of a classroom are such that power relations are more symmetrically distributed (Gutierrez & Larson 1994).

This data example is representative of another pattern that emerged from the analysis of the literacy activities Daisy conducted with her class. The teacher makes frequent attempts to situate the students as active social subjects in the creation and elaboration of this text (and most others) and discussion on war. For example, in her initiation in line 1 ("Using your ideas, how could we extend this sentence?"), she appears to perform a "student subjectification"[2] as she asks the students to draw from their own ideas to expand and elaborate on Esteban's initial sentence. Daisy's act of having a student come up with the initial "seed sentence" in the first place was also an act of student subjectification. Compare this to how Guillermo began his lesson around the word "war": "For us, Salvadorans, this word, 'war,' is very heavy for us. To a Costa Rican, to hear 'war' does not cause any effect. In our country..." In this example from Guillermo's classroom (Example 1, above), the students were not invited to contribute to the teacher's mostly one-sided discussion on the sociopolitical issues surrounding the war in El Salvador. Most of this context was provided by the teacher.

Daisy handles this differently. Daisy performs a student subjectification again in line 13 when she asks Gloria, who has suggested they add the words "El Salvador" to their evolving text, "Where should I put it?" In this way, Daisy encourages her students to contribute to the content and form of the growing text. Finally, at the end of the third and final IRE segment in this discourse sequence (see lines 60-65, below), Daisy again acts to subjectify students as she tells them what she intends they do with this text: "Using your ideas, and discussion, we're going to develop this...We're going to talk more about this and extend the paragraph."

As this discourse sequence continues, Daisy asks the students the difference between their original sentence (*"La guerra no es buena"*/"War is not good") and their new sentence (*"La guerra de El Salvador no es buena porque ha destruido mucho el país"*/"The war of EL Salvador is not good because it has destroyed the country much"):

31 Daisy:	Which sentence conveys more meaning	I III
32	and information?	
33 Farabundo:	With the first version, I didn't know what part	R
34	of the world it pertained to.	
35 Gloria:	The last version is more complex.	R
36 Daisy:	(xx) because (xx) there is a reason.	E
37	We could talk for months on this reality.	

Analysis of the data further revealed that it is not only Daisy who positions students as active social subjects, but the students themselves have begun to do so, through assuming at first resistant, and then agentive, stances (against hegemonic pedagogical practice, not against Daisy, necessarily[3]). Farabundo strikes a resistant stance when he suggests (lines 2-3) that they expand their sentence to read *"La guerra no es buena porque ha destruido mucho el país."* Gloria also takes up a stance of resistance (in line 12) when she suggests, unsolicited, that they add "El Salvador" to the sentence to provide more specificity. Finally, in lines 33-34 and 35, above, Farabundo and Gloria assume resistant stances again as they respond to Daisy's question. Farabundo says that "With the first version, I didn't know what part of the world it pertained to" even though he was the author of the original sentence. Gloria notes, "The last version is more complex." It is important to remember that these two students were considered, academically, to be marginally "average" by their previous teacher. Gloria would rarely verbally participate in classroom literacy activities under Guillermo. She would usually quietly follow Guillermo's instructions. Yet in this setting both of these students appear to be active, which does not follow dominant hegemonic pedagogical patterns.

After Daisy's comments in line 37, above, the students begin to share some of their experiences with war in El Salvador. And they do so at some length:

38	Students:	((Begin to share personal stories about their	R
39		experiences with the war in El Salvador.))	
40	Gloria:	We were out in a car. With my sister. I was eight.	R
41		The soldiers threw a bomb at the car.	
42		All the people died, including four children.	
43		They took me to the hospital. I still have this mark here.	
44		((She indicates a scar on her head	
45		just above the hair line.))	
46		I was all bloody on my face. My sister lived.	
47		The driver was yelling at the soldiers,	
48		"Don't throw bombs at me! I'm...(xx)...(xx)..."	
49		But they did it anyway.	
50	Students:	((Talk about the death squads, the differences	R
51		between the FMLN and the Salvadoran government,	
52		and the military's practice of "forced conscription."))	
53	Gloria:	It's getting worse again. Everyone is armed.	R
54	Daisy:	People have had to re-arm to protect themselves.	R
55		There are on-going skirmishes, even though	
56		the elections are approaching.	
57		There are personal stories, but I think we have to look	E
58		at larger processes. Before the semester is over, we're	
59		going to get an update from *Siempre* on the Salvadoran	
60		situation. Using your ideas, and discussion, we're going	
61		to develop this.	

62		((Referring to the sentence they wrote about war	
63		in El Salvador:))	

64		We're going to talk more about this,	
65		and extend the paragraph.	

66	Samuel:	My brothers, cousins, were all on the left.	R
67		They're all finished now.	

Daisy's students position themselves as active social subjects as they begin to assume agentive stances in their responses. In lines 38-52, through their elaborated sharing of experiences with war and violence in El Salvador, the students are playing a much more significant role in the creation of classroom knowledge than they had previously, or than is indicative of traditional, teacher-centered classrooms. In lines 66-67, Samuel assumes an agentive stance as he continues sharing his experiences ("My brothers, cousins, were all on the left. They're all finished now") even after Daisy has attempted to "evaluate" and wrap up the discussion for the evening (lines 66-67: "We're going to talk more about this and extend the paragraph"). The time has slipped past 9p.m. and it is genuinely time to go home, but Samuel continues to share his experiences with Daisy and me in dealing with the army and the FMLN in El Salvador as the rest of his classmates, of their own accord, begin to pack up and leave. Daisy does not stop him. Samuel continues to eagerly share with us even after we have walked out into the parking lot and are standing next to our cars, ready to go home. Eventually Samuel is satisfied, and leaves for home himself.

There is an important point to be made here, which is high-lighted in this case by Samuel's extended agentive stance—which began in the classroom and ended in the parking lot. To assume a conformist, resistant or agentive stance while one is studying with a particular teacher is not necessarily to assume one of these stances *against* that teacher. The way I have operationalized my coding, one assumes a particular stance in relation to hegemonic pedagogical practices.[4] In the case of Guillermo, it appeared as if he was attempting to maintain hegemonic pedagogical practices brushed with a veneer of Freirean language. Daisy seems to be attempting to implement a form of counter-hegemonic pedagogical practice (which is the goal of Freirean pedagogy). Nadia (the students' third teacher), as I will argue in the following chapter, has both hegemonic and counter-hegemonic pedagogical practices awkwardly co-existing simultaneously in her classroom. When a student takes up a "resistant" or "agentive" stance during one of Daisy's or Nadia's lessons, it is not necessarily in opposition to their practice, unless they begin to teach hegemonically. In Daisy's case, she appears, rather, to be *encouraging* students to assume resistant and agentive stances against hegemonic pedagogical practices and often positions them herself as active social subjects, so that they might more easily take up those stances.

Example 8
A Geo-political Text

I was unable to obtain a final version of the text Daisy's students began to create in Example 7, above. I was, however, fortunate enough to have the following text shared with me on another occasion during the same month. I was told that this text grew from a similar politically-oriented discussion on El Salvador, although in this case with a focus on international politics, economics and NAFTA (the North American Free Trade Agreement between Mexico, the United States and Canada), instead of war. The text was dictated and expanded by the students (as was the text in Example 7) and written on the board by Veronica, a student. The teacher watched and facilitated. I include it as an example to show the type of texts that grew out of the elaborated and dialogic thematic discussions regularly held between Daisy and her students. This text, and other similar texts, became the basis of this class' study of written Spanish.

Los paises del 3er mundo nunca se van a superar porque este país no los deja. La guerra en El Salvador es un ejemplo de eso. La pobreza de ese país es causada por los EEUU. Los EEUU sabe que con México tiene el futuro, por eso quiere el tratado de libre comercio. México tampoco se supera, este país impide la posibilidad de progreso a otros países. Un ejército nunca puede (XX) con la organización de un pueblo.

The countries of the 3rd World are never going to advance, because this country will not let them. The war in El Salvador is an example of this. The poverty of this country is caused by the United States. The United

States knows that it has a future with Mexico, therefore it wants NAFTA. Mexico is not improving either, this country impedes the possibility for progress of other countries. An army can never (xx) against the organization of the people.

It appeared that through discursive interactions like the one presented in Example 7, and through the collective production and use of relevant sociopolitical texts such as the one in Example 8, Daisy's students began positioning themselves as critical agents in this emerging counter-hegemonic discourse community. These discourse samples, it bears repeating, are representative of patterns of social practice in the classroom that emerged during my analysis of the larger corpus of data.

Example 9
Fill in the Blank

In this discourse sequence, the class is studying the pronunciation and written differences in Spanish between the syllables *ge-gi, je-ji* and *gue-gui.* Daisy and her students talk about the fact that if you do not insert the letter "u" between the letters that form the syllables *ge* and *gi*, they are pronounced the same as *je-ji*, which creates some linguistic difficulties.

Daisy has written the following words, with blank spaces in them, on the board: ___tarra, ___llermo, ___nete, ___rafa, ___rra, a___rrido, a___la, ___nebra, ___latina, ___rrilla, tra___, ___gante, ___neroso, ___tomate, mane___, a___tado and ca___ta. She has also made, and placed on the students' tables, small rectangles of paper with the lower case syllables *ge, gi, je, ji, gue* and *gui* on them. In this activity, Daisy shares with me, the students' task is to tape the rectangles of paper on the board in the appropriate space to complete a desired word. As the discourse sequence begins below, Samuel, Esteban and Farabundo have already created the words "*guerra*" ("war"), "*guitarra*" ("guitar") and "*ginebra*" ("gin"), respectively.

1	Gloria:	[(((Is holding a piece of paper with "gui" printed on	I	I
2		it up to one of the blank spaces on the board.))		
3		[I put it here?		

| 4 | Samuel: | No. Where it says "Guillermo." | R |
| 5 | | There. There above. That part there. | |

| 6 | Esteban: | Yes. | R |

| 7 | Gloria: | ((She tapes the card with its mate on the | R |
| 8 | | board, creating "Guillermo.")) | |

| 9 | Samuel: | [((To Gloria and Daisy:)) | E/I II |

| 10 | | [You have to use a capital letter with names. | |

| 11 | Daisy: | You're right. Next time, I'll correct it. | E/R |

In this discourse example we continue to see a wide variety of IRE patterns. There are three IR pairings (IV and VII, below), one IRR sequence (VIII, below), one IRRR sequence (I, above), an I E/R pairing (III, below), an E/I E/R pairing (II, above) and an IIEEE sequence (V, below). These IRE patterns are very flexible, and indicate, as in the previous data sample, the use of a "responsive" as opposed to "recitation" teaching script. Further, in this discourse sequence, the students not only respond to initiations (lines 4-5, 6, 7-8, 15), but also begin initiations (lines 1, 12, 16, 21, 24) and provide evaluations (lines 9-10, 18, 19, 20); that is, students freely assume all the roles (initiators, respondents and evaluators) within the IRE pattern. This free assumption of positions, in addition to the flexible nature of the IRE patterns, appears to define this as a conversation-like interaction where there is much back and forth turn-taking, and a more even distribution of classroom power. The interaction continues:

| 12 | Farabundo: | Does it say *"cajita"* there? | I III |

| 13 | Daisy: | Very good. I was thinking *"cajeta,"* a sweet. | E/R |
| 14 | | But very good. That's good. | |

Daisy continues to use student subjectification to position students as active social subjects. She does so in line 11, above ("You're right. Next time, I'll correct it"). This utterance was labeled as an evaluation/response, because Daisy is performing both of these functions. First, she acknowledges Samuel's point that proper names begin with capital letters, thus subjectifying his valid grammatical knowledge ("You're right..."). Second, she is exonerating Gloria—who had a "gui," and not a "Gui," syllable rectangle to choose from in completing the word "guillermo" on the board. And Daisy notes *her* own error ("Next time, I'll correct it").

Daisy performs another student subjectification in lines 13-14, above, as she evaluates and responds to Farabundo's question in line 12 ("Does it say *'cajita'* there?"). Daisy acknowledges and positively evaluates Farabundo's guess by saying, "Very good." But she is also being self-evaluative, as in the previous example with Samuel and Gloria, for she says that she was thinking of another word, but that Farabundo's word was unique and also correct within the given assignment parameters ("I was thinking *'cajeta,'* a sweet. But very good. That's good").

Daisy continues discursively positioning students as active social subjects through "student subjectification" below, in line 17. Esteban is testing the syllable/word pair *"ji"* and "___*gante*" (line 15), and asks for feedback: "How's this?" (line 16). Instead of evaluating his guess herself, Daisy turns the job of evaluation over to the students with a new initiation. She asks the group, "What's your opinion?" By positioning students as evaluators, Daisy is subjectifying them as actors with valuable knowledge and opinions.

15	Esteban:	((Makes the word: jigante.))	R	IV
16	Esteban:	How's this?	I	V
17	Daisy:	What's your opinion?	I (E->Ss)	
18	Gloria:	It goes with the "j."	E	
19	Samuel:	With the "g."	E	
20	Esteban:	With the "j."	E	

Students, during this discourse sequence, also repeatedly self-position as active social subjects through assuming agentive stances in their responses and evaluations. Both Samuel and Esteban take up agentive stances in lines 4-6 as they assist Gloria in making the word *"guillermo."* In these responses ("No. Where it says *'Guillermo.'* There. There above. That part there," and "Yes"),

Samuel and Esteban act more as teachers than classmates—or, as Freire puts it, "students/teachers" (1970). Student counter-hegemonic and self-redefining actions such as these appear to be an acceptable part of the evolving counter-discourse of this class-room. Samuel continues in this agentive mode in line 10 as he ad-vises Gloria that, "You have to use capital letters with names." Gloria, Samuel and Esteban also assume agentive stances in lines 18 ("It goes with the 'j'"), 19 ("With the 'g'") and 20 ("With the 'j'"), as they take on the task Daisy has given them in line 17 ("What's your opinion?") of evaluating Esteban's proto-word *"jigante."*

As this discourse sequence continues, Daisy comes in with an evaluation, and further initiation when she says, "With the 'g'." Esteban changes *"jigante"* to *"gigante"* ("giant"). Smiling, and seemingly unfazed by the correction, and comments, "Hey, I've done four, and I didn't even come to class yesterday. The interac-tion continues:

21	Gloria:	[((To Daisy, in the informal *tú* form:))	I VI
22		[Daisy, will you do me a favor?	
23	Daisy:	Yes. What?	R
24	Gloria:	Will you let me copy the words into my notebook?	I VII
25	Students:	((Laugh because they know of Daisy's preference not	R
26		to have her students copy from the board.))	
27	Daisy:	Yes.	R
28		But first let's read them.	I VIII

The final agentive stance assumed by a student in this discur-sive interaction occurs when Gloria asks Daisy the question (line 22, above), "Daisy, will you do me a favor?" For a student to make a request of their teacher is not an agentive act in-and-of-itself, but doing so in the familiar *tú* form in Spanish, which she did, (*"Daisy, ¿me haces un favor?"*) is. I had never noted the use of the *tú* form toward Guillermo, and this was the first time I had heard it used toward Daisy. From my experience as a researcher and bilingual classroom teacher, speaking to one's teacher as if they were a close friend or family member in the *tú* form, although it does happen, is not the acceptable norm in most Spanish language classrooms. This would be even less acceptable in a classroom defined by a hegemonic pedagogy that views students as subordinate to teachers. Yet after this incident, it soon became commonplace to hear Daisy's students comfortably using this more intimate form of the language with her. The fact that Gloria felt comfortable enough to speak in this way to Daisy may indicate that Gloria is beginning to see herself as a legitimate social actor in this classroom.

Through subtle ("You have to use capital letters with names," line 10) and not-so-subtle ("What's your opinion?", line 17) discursive interactions with each other and with their teacher, the students in this classroom appear to be slowly co-creating a counter-hegemonic discourse community where they, their opinions and their actions are valued.

Example 10
Words that Begin with "H"

In this discourse sequence, Daisy is trying to elicit examples of words from the students that begin with the letter "h"—which is silent in Spanish. She prompts, "Let's think about what's in the kitchen." After a student suggests a word different from what she had been thinking, Daisy says, "I made a mistake. I was thinking what we call a refrigerator in Argentina, '*heladora*'." As before, this appears to be a form of self-evaluation, self-critique, as Daisy acknowledges the possibility of alternative answers to the question of items that begin with the letter "h" one can find in the kitchen and different vocabularies from different Latin American countries (Daisy is from Argentina, and her students are from El Salvador and Mexico). This discourse sequence begins with the instance of student subjectification just described—with the teacher valuing a student response over her own. It continues as Daisy asks the students a grammatical question:

1	Daisy:	How do we know when to put an "h"?	I I
2		Let's get more examples.	

3	Ignacio:	[((Holds up the *Silabario Hispano Americano*))	
4		[There are lots of examples in this book.	R
5	Daisy:	Oh, good.	E
6		But let's come up with examples ourselves.	I II
7		((She writes on board:))	
8	•	[*helados / elados*	
9	Ignacio:	[((Reads as Daisy writes this	R
10		on the board.))	
11	Daisy:	Silvia, how do we know? Can we?	I III
12		We can't. There is no way. We just have to	R
13		learn the words (([that begin with the silent "h"])).	
14		Like Ignacio said, the only way to know them is to	R
15		read them.	
16		When the "h" is in the middle of a word,	R
17		the "c" takes it up.	

As in the previous two examples, an analysis of this discourse sequence reveals that a relaxed IRE pattern is the norm, rather than the exception, in Daisy's classroom. In this example, we find IRE, IRR and IRRR sequences. While not as relaxed as in Examples 7 and 9 above, students nonetheless continue to have frequent opportunities to participate in and generate classroom talk and to produce elaborated speech.

Further, Daisy continues to subjectify students and their knowledge in her initiations, responses and evaluations within those IRE sequences. She begins to do so in her initiation in lines 1 and 2 above ("How do we know when to put an 'h'?" and "Let's get some examples"), as she draws on students' knowledge of the Spanish language, usage and grammar. After Ignacio tries to focus attention away from student knowledge in favor of knowledge from an official text (lines 3-4), Daisy performs a quick evaluation (line 5), "Oh, good," and then refocuses on, and subjectifies, *student* knowledge (line 6), "But let's come up with examples ourselves." In IRE cluster III, Daisy asks (line 11) and then answers (lines 12-17) her own question. This is, in essence, a monologue on her part. But even during this monologue, Daisy continues to locate her students as active rather than passive social subjects. She does this in lines 14-15 when she draws on, in responding to her own initiation, expertise that Ignacio shared earlier, "Like Ignacio said, the only way to know them is to read them." That is, the only way to know which words begin with the letter "h" in Spanish is to memorize them. Daisy performs her final act of student subjectification in lines 20-21, below. In this evaluation, she once again invokes Ignacio as expert, and says, "Let me sum-up what you said, Ignacio. And tell me if I'm wrong." In these two sentences, Daisy not only draws on student knowledge and experience, but also allows that *she* might be incorrect. The sequence continues with the teacher asking:

18	Daisy:	And what does that make?	I IV
19	Ignacio:	The "ch."	R
20	Daisy:	Let me sum-up what you said, Ignacio.	E
21		And tell me if I'm wrong.	
22		The "h" goes at the beginning of a word,	I V
23		but[=	
24	Ignacio:	[but with a "c" you say it[=	R
25	Daisy:	[=it makes it a "ch"	R
26	Ignacio:	But if it's in a proper name, you don't pronounce the "h."	R

During this discourse sequence, Ignacio assumes both conformist and agentive stances. In lines 3-4, discussed briefly above, Ignacio, in response to the teacher's initiation, assumes a conformist stance when he holds up his *Silabario Hispano Americano* and suggests that, "There are lots of examples in this book." Ignacio, in this instance, elevates the knowledge of this official text over his own or his classmates'. Instead of trying to generate words that begin with "h," he opts for the official knowledge of the *silabario*. Here he is assuming a conformist stance. But the situation is not quite that simple.

Under Guillermo, this *silabario* served to objectify Ignacio. It solidified his "otherness" from the rest of the students by setting him apart from them. Even though he was in Guillermo's class, he did not "know enough," according to the teacher, to participate in regular classroom instruction all of the time. He was receiving "separate instruction," with the *silabario* serving as tutor. This book was the tangible object of Ignacio's internal exile within the classroom. Ignacio, however, also *resisted* through his *silabario*. He would frequently ignore classroom performance requests made of him by Guillermo in favor of working quietly, and alone, with this book. Ignacio would also resist by reading words and syllables from this text in conspiratorial asides to me when he was to be performing other tasks.

Months later, in Daisy's classroom, does Ignacio's suggestion that the class look in *Sialbario Hispano Americano* for examples of words that begin with the letter "h" constitute a conformist stance that potentially reinvokes his objectification and "separate instruction" under Guillermo? Largely, it does. But Ignacio's *silabario* may have also come to represent a "safe harbor" for him in rough seas, a place into which he can retreat when he feels the need. In this sense, Ignacio's *silabario* also served as a resource for him. When he wanted to find something that he could read, that he could have success at, he would go there. When Ignacio is asked to come up with words that begin with the letter "h," he turns first to his *silabario*, a text which has not only been the source of his otherness, but also a place to turn to for occasional success.

In the IRRR sequence that ends this discourse example (lines 22-26, above), Ignacio assumes agentive stances in line 24 ("...but with a 'c' you say it...") and line 26 ("But if it's a proper name, you don't pronounce the 'h'") as he co-constructs knowledge with the teacher. Through this series of interwoven and overlapping utterances, Ignacio and Daisy review several rules to keep in mind when working with the letter "h" in Spanish:

1) The "h" usually goes at the beginning of a word;
2) When in the middle of a word it is usually combined with the letter "c" to form the new letter "ch"; and,
3) You do not pronounce the "h" if it is in a proper name.

Whether or not these "rules" are completely correct or not, the fact that they are jointly elaborated by teacher and student, and that Ignacio feels free to do this, demonstrates that Ignacio is assuming an agentive stance against traditional, hegemonic pedagogical practices, and that he is coming to see himself, and act, in a new way.

Throughout these three representative examples, it has been shown how Daisy frequently attempts to position her students as active social subjects. Elaborated and lengthy dialogues, with back-and-forth turn-taking, around issues of social, political and personal import (as in Example 7), are common. Through classroom discussions, and through more formal activities and lessons (Examples 9 and 10), Daisy encourages the *co*-construction of academic and sociocultural knowledge in her classroom. Guillermo's former students have moved from conforming and resisting hegemonic pedagogical practices to resisting and acting agentively against them.

Sociopolitical Critical Student Agency: Going Beyond the Classroom

Besides the forms of academic critical student agency detailed above, there was also student agency evidenced in the *sociopolitical* sphere outside of class for this group of learners. Although its development was limited, and did not grow to the same levels that students' academic critical agency did, it was nonetheless present. This growth did not begin under Guillermo, where it was noted by the program coordinators that his students were among the least likely to participate in on-going sociopolitical events and functions *Siempre* would organize—such as fund raisers or community gatherings, or in outside events like rallies, marches or political campaigns. Under Daisy, this slowly began to change.

For example, Gloria, after much encouragement from classmates and Daisy, agreed to serve on the *Siempre* Student Council as a representative from her classroom. The Council met once a week and was charged with making important decisions regarding the program's funding, expenditures, governance and activities to be pursued within the community. As a council member, Gloria was to attend the regular weekly meetings held on site, take notes and report back to her constituents—the other students in Daisy's literacy class. She fulfilled her duties with pride, diligence and ea-gerness. It was later revealed that her taking of notes, and her re-porting back to the class, represented the first time this novice lit-erate had been called upon to use her slowly developing literacy skills to such an advanced degree. This was a risk for her. What if she had not been able to actually *take* notes? What if she had not been able to report back accurately *from* her notes to the class? What if she was not taken seriously by the other Council members because she was an *Alfa* student?[5] Gloria met the challenge, took a chance and succeeded. And she was regularly recognized for her efforts by her classmates and teacher.

On another occasion, one of Daisy's most soft-spoken, yet academically advanced students, Veronica, attended a commu-nity organized pro-immigrants' rights march and rally that *Siempre* and the teachers had been encouraging students to attend. This event was at the beginning of what has now become a full frontal assault on documented and undocumented immigrants' rights in California—beginning with Proposition 64 and culminating in Propositions 187, 209, 227 and the state and national dismantling of affirmative action. Many students expressed fear during class-room and community discussions leading up the march and rally. There was a concern that it would be risky to attend such an event. The students were in a foreign country, many of them did not have documentation and there would be police and media present. Possibly as a result of these discussions and fears, *Siem-pre* student participation at this event was very low. The coordi-nator, the teachers (except for Guillermo and Nadia), *Siempre* ac-tivists who were not part of the education program, and I, did at-tend. And so did Daisy's student Veronica. Not only did Veron-ica attend and walk in the march, but she soon found herself—timidly at first, but then more loudly and vigorously—raising her fist and chanting, along with the crowd of more than 10,000 mostly Latina/o marchers, "*El pueblo, unido, ¡jamás será vencido!*" ("The people, united, will never be defeated!"), among other chants and slogans. This was the first time I had seen Veronica, in over five months of field work, ever raise her voice above a sub-dued conversational tone, not to mention raise her fist! It was a dramatic manifestation of critical student agency.

To triangulate these findings of the formation of a counter-hegemonic discourse community, and the resultant development of both academic and sociopolitical critical student agency, it is useful to look at other forms of data and other interactions. In the next section, therefore, interview data will be reviewed and analyzed to determine if what students were *saying* about their experiences was in line with what I observed happening discursively in and outside of their classroom.

Agency or Conformism: Which Lessons Take?

Despite the many instances of resistance and agency against hegemonic pedagogical practices discursively exhibited by these students, during formal and informal interviews at which Daisy was not present, these learners seemed to reinvoke many procedural aspects of their former hegemonic practices under Guillermo. For example, during an informal interview half-way through Daisy's tenure as his teacher, Juan demonstrates his resistance to her attempted instantiation of counter-hegemonic pedagogical practices. He tells me, "We want a more practical teacher. One who comes in...puts some stuff on the board, teaches us, and that's it."

On a cool evening in late December of 1993, approximately a month after Juan's comment, all of the students were interviewed by Gregorio, the new *co*-coordinator of the ESL/literacy project. At the time of this particular interview, Daisy was not present. Gregorio wanted to gauge the students' level of satisfaction with the program, how they thought they were progressing and how the program might be improved. Portions of this interview, at which both Daisy's and the other Spanish literacy instructor's (Nadia) students were present, is presented below as Example 11.

Example 11
"During dictation, well, one learns the words":
An Interview with Students

1	Gregorio:	Do you think you've learned during your time
2		in this course? Or is the rhythm too slow for you?

3	Patricia:	It's slow, but we're advancing.
4		It's not the instructors' fault.

5		[It's because of this head I have, you know.
6		[(((She raps her closed fist three times on her head.))
7	Gregorio:	What are your favorite exercises?
8		What helps you learn the best?
9	Fernando:	Dictation.
10	Esteban:	Dictation.
11	Veronica:	During dictation, well, one learns the words.
12	Fernando:	When the teacher writes on the board,
13		one loses their fear.

During this interview, students predominately assume conformist stances toward hegemonic pedagogical practices. But these are conformist stances of different types. As Fernando, Esteban and Veronica voice their preference for dictation (lines 9-13, above) as the best type of classroom exercise (as opposed to, say, writing their own sentences, doing group or collaborative exercises or having classroom discussions), they are, at least to some extent, reinvoking hegemonic pedagogical practices and the hegemonic discourse community they co-created under Guillermo.

But an even stronger conformist stance is assumed by Patricia (in line 3), one of Nadia's students, at the beginning of the interview. In response to Gregorio's question, "Do you think you've learned during your time in this course? Or is the rhythm too slow for you?" Patricia comments, "It's slow, but we're advancing. But it's not the instructors' fault." She raps on her head three times with a closed fist and says, "It's because of this head I have, you know," as if to indicate that she is thick-headed. Through this discursive and gestural conformist stance, she positions herself as an passive social subject whose job it is to absorb information given to her by the teacher. But even at this passive job, she is unsuccessful. She is not learning. Her "thick head" is coming between her teacher's dissemination of facts and her brain's ability to absorb them.

This level of conformism is not evidenced in Fernando, Esteban and Veronica's voiced preference for "dictation" over some of the more interactional forms of learning they had been practicing under Daisy. Even though they may still prefer teacher dictation, these students are no longer actively embracing a vision of self that defines them as "empty"—as demonstrated in Patricia's comments above or as shared previously during their time with Guillermo ("From us comes nothing").

Finally, while Daisy's students are reinvoking dictation as a preferred form of classroom practice, we do not know exactly how they would like to see that form implemented. They could be conceiving of "dictation" in a very different way now, in a way that involves more student participation, editing and discussion. They might now react by assuming resistant and agentive stances to a teacher dictation that was handled in the former way. Or they might not. This we cannot know for certain. Although, as we follow Fernando, Esteban and Gloria into their next classroom, and next discourse community with Nadia, the answers to some these questions do become more evident.

The interview continues as Gregorio asks the literacy students about their feelings regarding the class discussions of the generative themes that delineate their units of study. These dialogues are seen by the coordinators of this Freirean-oriented program as central in the development of student sociopolitical consciousness.

14 Gregorio: The theme, the word discussion, does it help? Is it important?

15 Esteban: Well, you know, sometimes we spend 40 minutes
16   —half the time [discussing the theme].
17   Maybe we could be learning other things.
18   We could talk about the word more quickly.

19 Carlos: The teacher should say what the word is.
20   But that's it.

If we take the Freirean practice of centralizing discussion of sociopolitical issues in classrooms to be counter-hegemonic, then Esteban and Carlos (who is a student of Nadia's) assume conformist stances toward hegemonic pedagogical practices (lines 15-20) in their responses to Gregorio's question. These political discussions, according to Esteban, take up too much time that could be better spent in other ways (line 17: "Maybe we could be learning other things"). Carlos puts it even more bluntly (lines 19-20) when he says, "The teacher should say what the word is. But that's it." In other words, according to Carlos, if the word and theme being studied is "war," the teacher should tell the students, "This word says 'war'," and there should be no sociopolitical discussion whatsoever.[6]

If we focus, however, on Daisy's student Esteban, and how he is positioning himself in relation to hegemonic pedagogical practices, we notice something interesting. Esteban does not suggest that they do away with these sociopolitical discussions altogether, just that they proceed "more quickly" (line 18). In this way, he might not be calling for a full return to the hegemonic pedagogical practices of Guillermo—where, if there was a discussion at all, it was monological on the part of the teacher—but rather, a modification of the counter-hegemonic practices he has come to know and co-construct under Daisy.

In the conformist stances exhibited by Daisy's students during this interview, they seem to be, at the very least, "backsliding" from the more resistant and agentive stances observed during the representative discursive classroom interactions in Examples 7, 9 and 10, above. As they make clear during this interview, they want more dictation and less discussion. What accounts for this return to conformism over resistance or agency? And what does it mean? It could be that Fernando, Esteban and Veronica are in a period of adjustment. They, and their other classmates, have begun to see themselves, and to act, in very different ways than they used to. Maybe, as could have been the case with Ignacio and his *silabario* (Example 10, above), they are nostalgic for some aspects of their former hegemonic social practices. It could be that they are insecure about their new positioning as active social subjects. Again, we cannot know this for sure. But this might be one of the reasons for the students' shift toward conformism in this example.

Understanding Daisy's Classroom

As we consider these findings, a number of important questions come to mind. Is it through the actions of the students in conforming, resisting or acting agentively that a hegemonic versus counter-hegemonic discourse community is formed? Or is it through the actions of the teachers in positioning students as objects or subjects that one community over another is produced? All that can be said at this point is the following. First, as

Guillermo, in an engagement with hegemonic pedagogical practices, acted to position his students as objects (as passive social subjects), and as his students themselves acted to self-position alternately as conformists or resistors within these practices, they co-created a hegemonic discourse community. Further, it appeared that this discourse community inhibited the development of critical student agency. Second, as Daisy, in challenging hegemonic pedagogical practices (from a position of Freirean/critical pedagogy), acted to position these same students as active social subjects, and as her students themselves acted to self-position alternately as resistors or agents against hegemonic pedagogical practices, they co-created a *counter*-hegemonic discourse community. Further, it appeared that this latter discourse community fostered the development of critical student agency.

My analysis of the data from Daisy's classroom revealed that she would consistently position students as active social subjects, and legitimate their academic and other forms of knowledge. Daisy consistently encouraged her students to draw on themselves and one another as legitimate providers of assistance, and to promote a vision of students as academic and sociopolitical change agents. Through discussions, activities and lessons of various sorts, it she encouraged the *co*-construction of academic and sociocultural knowledge in her classroom. It also became apparent that while reluctant at first, students began to take up these roles and *self*-position as agents versus conformists to the hegemonic pedagogical order. Daisy and her students jointly produced a counter-hegemonic discourse community, and set of pedagogical practices, that valued and sought to develop critical student agency.

This chapter presented findings that a counter-hegemonic discourse community was the form of social interaction that was dominant in the classroom of Daisy Contreras and her students, and how this community fostered the development of critical student agency. And it was demonstrated, through a critical discourse analysis, how this pedagogical practice was slowly and discursively constructed over time between the teacher and her students. It was also shown, however, that this was not a linear, fully successful, or completed process. Students were still struggling with where to locate themselves along the hegemonic/counter-hegemonic continuum, and what exact form they wanted their classroom practice to take.

The following chapter, "Creating the World through the Word: Practicing Counter-Hegemony," will focus on the social practices of Nadia Monterey and her students. These students were, for the most part, the same students that studied under Daisy. Through an analysis of regular discursive interactions in Nadia's classroom during literacy activities, the nature and variety of social interactions in which students and teacher engaged, and what this meant for the further development, maintenance or dissolution, of critical student agency, will be identified.

Notes

1. These specific words and sentences, drawn from field notes, were actually used in Guillermo's and Daisy's classrooms, respectively.

2. Teachers perform acts of "student subjectification" when they attempt to discursively position students as active social subjects.

3. More on Daisy's pedagogical practice, and its relation to hegemonic pedagogical practices, resistance and agency, below.

4. Again, hegemonic pedagogical practices are teacher and student acts which follow the "banking" pedagogy model described by Freire (1970, 1985) and the "recitation" pedagogy model elaborated by Gutierrez (1992). Within these hegemonic pedagogical practices, the classroom is a teacher-centered place where information is "transmitted" from "all-knowing" teacher to "empty" students.

5. There was a not unfounded concern among the students of the two Spanish literacy classes that the ESL students looked down upon them because the could not yet read or write proficiently in Spanish, while the ESL students, for the most part, could.

6. Refer to Examples 1 and 7 for Guillermo and Daisy's different approaches to using socio-political themes in a classroom context.

References

Freire, P. 1970. *Pedagogy of the Oppressed*. Rámos, M., trans. New York: Continuum.

_____ . *Politics of Education*. South Hadley: Bergin & Garvey.

Gutierrez, K. 1991a. "Coding Sheet. The Social Contexts of Literacy Study." Kris Gutierrez, principal investigator. An unpublished document. University of California, Los Angeles.

_____ . 1991b. "The Effects of Writing Process Instruction on Latino Children." Paper presented at the Annual Meeting of the American Educational Research Association. Chicago, Illinois.

_____ . "A Comparison of Instructional Contexts in Writing Process Classrooms with Latino Children." *Education and Urban Society* 24: 244-262.

Gutierrez, K. and Larson, J. 1994. "Language Borders: Recitation as Hegemonic Discourse." *International Journal of Educational Reform* 3: 22-36.

Creating the World through the Word: Practicing Counter-Hegemony

In cultural synthesis, the actors who come from 'another world' to the world of the people do so not as invaders. They do not come to teach or to transmit or to give anything, but rather to learn with the people, about the peoples' world.

—Paulo Freire (1970:181)

This chapter focuses on the forms of social interaction that appeared to foster the development of critical student agency in the classroom of Nadia Monterey and her students. Through a presentation and discussion of the findings, it will be shown how the teacher and students in this classroom collectively produced a learning community that was comprised of both "hegemonic" *and* "counter-hegemonic" discourse, and how this community continued to foster the critical student agency that its students began experiencing and then co-constructing under their former teacher, Daisy. To situate the findings and discussion that comprise the majority of this chapter, I will first begin with brief descriptions of several of Nadia's students and the physical and pedagogical spaces they occupied at *Siempre*.

The Students and The Classroom

Nadia's class, which was formed when the two former *Alfa* classes were reconfigured, is composed of approximately five students. Fernando, who studied with Nadia before the class reorganization, is a young Mexican man in his mid-twenties. He and I already know each other in passing because his daughter attended pre-kindergarten at the neighborhood school down the street, where I taught. Fernando is friendly and gregarious, and according to Nadia and Daisy, one of the most academically advanced students in the class. Joining him from Daisy's class are Esteban, Gloria and Juan. Veronica, Ignacio, Farabundo and Samuel attend at first, but eventually leave the program to pursue second jobs in the evenings.

The general physical location of Nadia's new *Alfa 2* classroom is the same. It is one of the classes that are held in a store-front that *Siempre* leases. However, not all of the classrooms—created when the project installed removable walls to sub-divide the space—are the same. Some of these new rooms are larger than others, and at least one, a small room located close to the entrance, serves as the through-way to the other classrooms. Nadia Monterey and her students occupy this room. While it is equipped with two large tables, a new white erase board and a good number of plastic resin chairs, it is still little more than a glorified hallway. Three of the four classes, their students, teachers and visitors, have to pass through Nadia's classroom to get to their own. The result of this lack of architectural forethought is that Nadia and her students experience frequent interruptions as other students are either going to, or leaving from, their classrooms. Nadia and her students, however, make due.

In Nadia's classroom, there is a return a more teacher-centered pedagogical philosophy, as evidenced in the use of teacher-generated syllables, words and short texts that adorn the walls and board. As under their first teacher, Guillermo, Nadia's preference is for rote memorization, drills and dictation. As she shares with her colleagues during one of the teacher training sessions, she supports the Freirean/"popular" approach, but has doubts as to how to reconcile it with her own pedagogy. During one of the teacher training sessions she asks, "I want to know something specific...How do I teach the syllables *ga, gue, gui, go, gu* with popular education?" The session facilitators do not provide any easy or quick answers for Nadia, for many basic elements of the teacher-centered/traditional approach are fundamentally at odds with the more student-centered and transformation-oriented Freirean approach.

Classroom activities under Nadia center mostly around the reading or copying of texts from the board that the teacher has selected. Yet Nadia's classroom is not the same as Guillermo's in several notable respects. While Nadia's overall pedagogical philosophy, and the exercises she has her students perform, are traditional, the *way* she allows these activities to unfold through social practices in the classroom is quite different. Nadia works at a slower pace, and in more of an unstructured way, than did Guillermo. Through interviews, and ethnographic observations during teacher planning meetings, I came to understand that this represents for Nadia a subtle form of *teacher* resistance to the orientation of the program. While she voices occasional support for the program's Freirean ideals, she is always quick to express her doubts about enacting those ideals, especially if they mean she has to do more "off-the-clock" planning or facilitate potentially unwieldy and lengthy classroom discussions of a political nature. As a self-described "non-political person," she shares with that she does not have much interest in this. So she resists. She resists by keeping sociopolitical classroom discussions largely perfunctory and minimal, by having students participate in traditional reading and copying exercises, and by not doing much planning. It seems as if, while not acting in an openly hostile way, her heart is not in the Freirean process.

But Nadia's actions, or *in*actions, seem to have some interesting effects. Her "hands-off" approach to lesson planning and classroom time/discourse management leave substantial "gaps" and "spaces" in the discourse of the classroom. When students are copying a text from the board in their notebooks, she gives them all the time they need to complete the task. When they are reading passages from the board in turn, she does not rush or frequently interrupt them. When she is dictating words to them, she takes her time. When Nadia's students need assistance in one of these tasks, she is not quick to help them. And so gaps and spaces develop in the classroom discourse. But this space is not left unfilled. It is the students themselves who fill these gaps and spaces. And they do so with their own talk and gesture. While Nadia is in charge of the selection of activities and topics, it appears that the *students* run many of the discursive interactions in the classroom. When one of their own has trouble decoding a word from the board, they help her sound it out. When a student has difficulty copying something into his notebook, a fellow student jumps in to assist.

Critical Student Agency Maintained:
Practicing Counter-Hegemony

Analysis of the data from literacy activities collected in Nadia's classroom revealed that a "counter-hegemonic discourse community" continued to be the prevailing form of social practice in this classroom. And this form of social practice appeared to continue to foster the development of critical student agency. Students who had begun to be socialized to counter-hegemonic practices under their previous teacher, Daisy—although not without contradictions—found a classroom environment under Nadia where they could maintain, and possibly further develop, their growing sense of selves as active social subjects, as critical agents, despite Nadia's use of traditional, teacher-centered exercises and philosophical orientation. The following discourse examples are representative of a pattern of student "objectification" *and* "subjectification" on the part of the teacher, and student "conformist," "resistant" *and* "agentive" stances on the part of the students. This pattern emerged from an analysis of the class' social practices within literacy activities.

The Discursive Positioning of Students as "Agents" in a Hegemonic/Counter-Hegemonic Setting

All of the following data examples surround one significant and typical activity that Nadia had her students engage in on an evening in March of 1994. The students and teacher had been informally and formally discussing the possibility of forming a "financial cooperative" over the previous two months. This grew out of a classroom discussion of different types of community work and solidarity when the class was studying the generative word "*comunidad*" ("community"). Nadia did some research and found a text she wanted her students to study that provided a definition and background information on "savings and lending cooperatives." Example 12, below, is the version of this text that Nadia wrote on the board (English translation is provided below the original text in Spanish). After Nadia writes the text on the board, she has her students begin to read the title and first paragraph in "round robin" fashion. In Example 13, Juan is reading the title of the text from the board, and then engages in an interaction over the text with his classmates. In Example 14, Gloria is reading from the first paragraph of the text, has trouble, and is assisted by Juan and Esteban. Finally, in Example 15, Fernando is reading. When he experiences difficulty, Juan, Esteban and Gloria offer their assistance.

Example 12
The "Cooperative" Text

cooperaTiva de ahorro y CrédiTo.[1]
Savings and Credit Cooperative[2]

EsTa es una agrupación de personas que se unen para ahorrar dinero y proporcionarse crédito a intereses razonables.

This is a group of people who unite to save money and offer credit at reasonable rates.

los miembros (socios) de esTa cooperaTiva de ahorro adquienen el hábito de ahorrar y se ayudan entre ellos mismos para resoluer problemas económicos.

The members of this savings cooperative become accustomed to the habit of saving, and they help each other resolve economic problems.

Esta cooperativa tiene el beneficio de presTar dineros con menos requisitos de los que piden un <u>Banco</u> y a un interés más baJo que el de los presTamisTas.

This cooperative has the benefit of being able to loan money with less requirements than a bank asks for, and at a lower interest than that of those who regularly loan money.

Example 13
"*Crédito dice, no créditos*": Assisting Juan

As Juan reads this five word title from the board ("*cooperaTiva de ahorro y CrédiTo*"/"Savings and Credit Cooperative"), his classmates watch and listen to him read, read along themselves and copy the sentence from the board into their notebooks.

| 1 | Juan: | ((Gets up, waits, and then begins to read | R I |
| 2 | | from the board.)) | |

3		$[{}^{\circ}co{}^{\circ}=$		
4		[((Taps board under syllable with ruler.))		
	Nadia/			
5	Gloria:	$[(xx)$		
6	Juan:	$[=co$		R
7		[((Taps.))		
8	Nadia:	((To Gloria:))		
9		*A bueno (xx).*		
10		Oh fine (xx).		
11	Juan:	$[per$ -	$[\underline{a}$	R
12		[((Taps.))	[((Taps.))	
13		$[tiva$		
14		[((Taps.))		
15		$[de$		
16		[((Taps.))		
17		$[a$		
18		[((Taps, lifts ruler, and pauses, moving the ruler		
19		back and forth under "*horros*," touching		
20		the board once.))		
21		((Long pause.))		
22		$[horros=$		
23		[((Taps.))		

In beginning to analyze this discourse sequence, we see that IRE patterns are not tightly restricted. Sequence I (lines 1-23, above), which begins with the teacher's much earlier initiation (not shown) that her students begin reading the passage in turn, takes the IRRR form. As Juan reads, there is no evaluation from Nadia, and he is given all the time he needs. IRE sequence II takes the E/I E/I R form as the teacher and another student evaluate and further initiate Juan in his reading (lines 24-32, below). Sequence III (lines 33-43, below) assumes an E/I E E E/I R pattern, and is distinguished by its openness. The E/I E RRRREREEIE discursive configuration that denotes the final IRE sequence in this discourse example (sequence IV, lines 44-70, below) is indicative of just how open and unrestricted the discourse patterns generally are in Nadia's classroom. These discursive interactions and IRE sequences are of note not only in that they are mostly filled with student talk, but also in that students assume *all roles* within the IRE sequence: initiations, responses and evaluations. The interaction continues:

24	Nadia:	Un huh.	E/I	II
25	Esteban:	[*Ahorro*	E/I	
26	Juan:	[=*y*	R	
27		[((Taps.))		
28		[*créditos*		
29		[((Taps twice.))		
30		[*Allí*		
31		[There		
32		[((Indicating his is finished reading that part.))		

One of the striking features about this discourse sequence is Nadia's lack of participation. Under Guillermo, the teacher was the most prominent participant in classroom talk. The social practices in Daisy's classroom were such that there was much discursive interaction between teacher and students, and the teacher was always an active participant. Nadia, however, is often not present in classroom discourse for long periods of time. In the example being presented here, Nadia set the agenda for what was to be studied by her students. She chose the topic ("cooperatives"), provided the pedagogical structure and format that would be used (reading round robin from the board) and selected a text ("lending and savings cooperatives"). Further, Nadia provided the *overall* "initiation" (I) for much of the discourse sequence from which Examples 13, 14 and 15 are drawn. For example, as Juan stands up, goes to the board, waits and then begins to read ("°*co*°..."), in lines 1-3 above, he is responding to the teacher's overall initiation that the students will read this specific text from the board.

Despite all of these elements over which Nadia has and exercises control, she is surprisingly absent from this seventy-one line interchange. The teacher has some brief side talk with Gloria as Juan begins to read (lines 5 and 8-10), in line 24 with a short (and incorrect) evaluation/initiation ("Un-huh"), and again in lines 66-67 as she attempts to initiate Juan and his classmates back into reading the text ("*Va::*") versus discussing how Juan had read it. But it is mostly the students who control this representative example of classroom talk. For example, as this discourse sequence continues with IRE segment III below (line 33), Fernando has noticed Juan's error (he has read "*créditos*" instead of "*crédito*"), and advises him of his mistake:

33	Fernando:	*Crédito dice n[o créditos.*	E/I III
34		Credit it says no[t credits.	
35	Gloria:	[*crédito*	E
36		((Laughs.))	
37	Juan:	((Looks back at the word "*crédito*," and brings	E
38		his hand with the ruler near his mouth, pensive.))	
39	Fernando:	*crédito - llevara la "s"*	E/I
40		credit - ((as if)) it took the "s"	
41		((or))	
42		credit - ((as if)) he took the "s" to it	
43	Juan:	*Créditos (xx)*	R

In this example, Nadia either does not notice Juan's mistake (in line 28), or chooses not to deal with it. But Juan's classmates do. Fernando assists Juan in lines 33-34 ("'*Crédito*' *dice, no* '*créditos*'"/"'Credit' it says, not 'credits'") and 39-42 ("*Crédito, llevara la* '*s*'"/"Credit, [as if] it took the 's'" or "Credit, [as if] he took the 's' to it"), and Gloria does so in line 35 ("*Crédito*"). Students bring both a level of conformity and agency to the social practices of this classroom. On the one hand, they accept the more traditional types of exercises Nadia has them do—recall the students' preference, in the interview at the end of Daisy's tenure, for dictation and copying, in Chapter 5. On the other hand, they assume agentive stances as they define *how* these exercises are implemented. Students are active social subjects who are often in charge of their own learning and can turn to each other for assistance instead of the teacher. They are not empty, but full, and are able to co-construct useful and valuable classroom knowledge together.

In this discourse sequence, many student agentive stances were noted (lines 25, 33-34, 35, 39-42, 44, 45-48, 54-57, 59-60, 61-65 and 69-70) as they assisted their peers, and themselves, in reading the teacher's passage from the board on their own. These agentive stances of assistance took several different forms: "sounding out," "reading it correctly," "summarizing/evaluating" and "reading for."

The following are examples of agentive stances of assistance in the form of "saying it correctly." In line 22, Juan reads *"horros"* where he should have read *"Ahorro."* First, Nadia mistakenly evaluates Juan's reading of the word in the affirmative (line 24: "Un-huh"). Then Esteban reads the word correctly, *"Ahorro"* (line 25). Although Juan responds to Esteban's evaluation/initiation by continuing to read (*"...y...créditos..."*), and does not attempt to re-read the word *"Ahorro,"* Esteban is still attempting to assist Juan in a way that agentively challenges hegemonic pedagogical practices. Under such practices, students are passive social subjects who receive meaning from the teacher, not active social subjects who create their own meaning or assist one another in generating meaning.

Fernando attempts to assist Juan in reading correctly another word he miss-read. In this case, the word is *"crédito."* Fernando says, *"'Crédito' dice, no 'créditos'"* ("'Credit,' it says, not 'credits'") in an evaluation/initiation (lines 33-34, above). Gloria attempts to assist Juan as well, and in an echo of Fernando's "saying it correctly" says, *"crédito"* (line 35). After some consideration on Juan's part (lines 37-38), he tries to read the word again, but makes the same mistake as before, and adds the "s," saying, *"créditos"* (line 43, above). In line 44 (below), Fernando uses the same "saying it correctly" technique of assistance by repeating, *"Crédito,"* in a more insistent tone. In lines 45-48, Juan appears to realize his mistake. His classmates' attempts to help him have been successful.

44	Fernando:	*Cr édito*	E/I IV
45	Juan:	*Pero (xx) la "s" que ya no [tenía*	E
46		But (xx) the "s" that it didn't alr[eady have	
47		((or))	
48		But (xx) the "s" that I didn't alr[eady have	
49		[((Begins to grin.))	R
50	All:	((Begin to laugh.))	R
51	Juan:	((Juan's grin turns into a big smile	R
52		as he too begins to laugh.))	
53	All:	((All laugh heartily.))	R
54	Esteban:	[*Cuando la lleva ¿no?*	E
55		[When he brought it—right ?	
56		((or))	
57		[When it was brought—right ?	
58	All:	[((Are still laughing.))	R
59	Gloria:	*Hay no la "s" que ya no tenga y se no [(xx)]*	E
60		((not translatable))	
61	Juan:	[*(xx]*	E
62		*Pero que la tenemos en [mente y=*	
63		but we have it in our [mind and=	
64		[((Pointing toward his	
65		head with the ruler.))	
66	Nadia:	[*Va::*	I
67		[Go ahead	
68		((Chuckles.))	
69	Juan:	=[*(xx)*	E
70		[((pointing toward the board))	
71		((Juan goes on to read the rest of the text.))	

Students also position themselves as active social subjects through the agentive stances they assume in assisting one another through the technique of "summarizing/evaluating." In this discourse sequence, we first see Fernando use "summarizing/evaluating" in lines 39-42 (above). Although Fernando and Gloria have tried to help Juan see his mistake, and how to fix it, and Juan is considering their advice, he has not yet understood his error. So Fernando tries again to help by summarizing what had happened when Juan read *"créditos"* instead of *"crédito."* Fernando says (here in English translation) either, "Credit, as if it took the 's'," or "Credit, as if he took the 's' to it" (lines 39-42). Not only is Fernando trying to explain to Juan and the other students what happened when Juan read *"créditos,"* but he also appears to be attempting to "save face" for Juan. It is my contention that Fernando is being purposefully ambiguous in the grammatical construction of his utterance here. When he uses the imperfect subjunctive to say, *"Crédito, llevara la 's',"* Fernando is choosing *not* to use an identifying pronoun like "he" (*"él"*) or "you" (*"tú"* or *"usted"*) when describing how Juan's error had taken place. Through this grammatical ambiguity, the door is left open for a redirection of fault away from Juan. Juan, *or the word itself*, could have put the "s" where it did not belong.

Under Nadia, the students would frequently use this grammatical "impersonalization of error" to draw attention away from reading mistakes their classmates had made. In Spanish it is not necessary to use personal pronouns. Unless they are contextually necessary, they are usually omitted. For example, one would normally say *"Estudiaron duro"* ("They studied hard") instead of *"Los alumnos de Nadia estudiaron duro"* (Nadia's students studied hard"), unless it was unclear who the subject of the sentence was. In this case, however, patterns in the data indicate that clarifying pronouns were purposefully omitted for reasons of face-saving. While these same students were studying under Guillermo, for example, they made concerted efforts to *use* pronouns to implicate each other in the commission of errors, as was the practice of the teacher. Instead of saying, *"Crédito, llevara la 's',"* they would often make comments such as, *"Tú leíste 'créditos,' pero dice 'crédito'"* ("You read 'credits,' but it says 'credit'"), or *"Así no es, no sabes leer"* ("That's not it, you don't know how to read").

In lines 45-48, above, Juan begins to understand his error, and assumes an agentive stance when he provides his own "summary/evaluation" of what happened. With his, *"Pero (xx) la 's' que ya no tenía"* ("But (xx) the 's' that it didn't already have" or "But (xx) the 's' that I didn't already have"), it appears he is attempting to metacognitively explain the processes that culminated in his mistake, as well as to grammatically impersonalize the mistake. Esteban (lines 54-57: *"Cuando la lleva, ¿no?"*—"When he brought it, right?" or "When it was brought, right?") and Gloria (lines 59-60: *"Hay no la 's' que ya no tenga y se no (xx)"*/not translatable) also both try to help Juan through the summarizing/evaluating and impersonalization of error assistance techniques. In the process, they assume agentive stances.

Throughout Example 13, Juan's classmates "scaffolded" (Rogoff 1990, 1991) Juan after he read a word from the passage incorrectly, giving him specific advice and clues as to what went wrong during his first read-through. The students' actions during this representative sequence mirrored classic elements of apprenticeship. Juan's classmates played an active role in organizing development. There was shared problem-solving. And there was a supportive structuring of the novice's efforts (Rogoff 1990). Furthermore, through this scaffolding and assistance, Nadia's students positioned themselves as active social subjects by assuming agentive stances, thus helping to produce and maintain a *predominately* counter-hegemonic discourse community, despite its surface trappings of "traditional" literacy exercises.

Example 14
Juan and Esteban Assist Gloria

In this example, Gloria is working her way through the sentence, *"Esta es una agrupación de personas..."* ("This is a grouping of people...") from the same text Juan was reading above on "cooperatives"—although she is farther along in the first section. As Gloria reads, Juan and Esteban interject to assist her when she has difficulties.

```
1   Gloria:     [e::↑                                    R
2               [(((Points at board with ruler.))

3               [(((Brings ruler back to touch chin.))
4               [(1.0)
```

5 Juan:	esta	E/I I
6 Gloria:	*e*	R
7	*es:: ta*	
8	(1.5)	
9 Esteban:	*e s*	I II
10 Gloria:	*e s*	R
11 Esteban:	*u[na*	I III
12 Juan:	*[una*	I
13 Gloria:	*una*	R
14	(0.8)	

In this discourse example, the IRE sequences are more re-stricted than in Example 13, above. They are still varied, however, and include IR, IIR, IRR and E/I E/I R patterns. Additionally, there are many opportunities for the student reader (Gloria) to receive input from her more skilled classmates (Juan and Esteban). During this interaction, there is no teacher participation whatsoever. It is completely controlled by the students. Student subjectification by the teacher is present only in that Nadia has set the boundaries for the activity within which the students are engaged, namely, reading round robin style from the board. Within these boundaries, however, students are actively creating a counter-hegemonic discourse community that values their knowledge and abilities.

The interaction continues with Esteban helping Gloria sound-out the *"a"* of *"agrupación."*

15 Esteban:	*a*	I IV
16 Gloria:	((Opens mouth as if to make the sound "ah."))	R
17	°*a::*°	
18 Esteban:	*gru [pa ción*	I V
19 Juan:	*[gru pa ción (.) ci[ón*	I
20 Gloria:	*[grupacióne*	R

| 21 | Juan/ | | |
| | Esteban: | *grupación* | E/I VI |

22	Gloria:	*[grupación*	
23		[((Taps ruler on the board twice as	
24		she reads *"grupación."*))	

As with the previous discourse sequence, the students continue to actively position themselves as subjects through agentive stances (lines 5, 9, 11, 12, 15, 18, 19, 21, 27, 33, 36, 37, 40 and 42). And these agentive stances continue to take the form of moves to assist one another through the techniques of "sounding out," "reading it correctly," "summarizing/evaluating" and "reading for." During this sequence, Esteban makes two attempts to help Gloria in her reading by sounding out part of the word she is trying to read. However, when Esteban (line 15) sounds-out the *"a"* of *"agrupación,"* it does not seem to help Gloria. She simply repeats his prompt (*"a"*), without reading the word *"agrupación."* Esteban's prompt in line 33 of *"pers::"* (from *"personas"*) does appear to help, as Gloria responds with *"pers:sonal"* (line 34). While not the exact word, it was close.

Juan and Esteban also employ the technique of saying correctly the word Gloria is trying to read, after she has attempted it on her own. This occurs with Juan and Esteban together in line 21. In line 20 Gloria tries to read *"grupación,"* but says *"grupacióne"* instead. Juan and Esteban say it correctly afterward with *"grupación"*— they do not say the *"a"* of *"agrupación"* because Gloria has already read that in line 17 (*"°a::°"*). Esteban uses this same technique as Gloria is trying to read the word *"personas,"* when, in line 36, he says, *"pers::onans."* Juan uses it both in line 37 (*"de personas"*) and in line 42 (*"personas"*).

These two techniques ("sounding out" and "reading it correctly") appear to be at least partially successful in assisting Gloria in reading the words with which she is having difficulty. These techniques also serve to position Juan and Esteban as active social subjects, as critical academic agents. Below, Gloria finishes reading the passage.

| 25 | Gloria: | *[d[e* | R |
| 26 | | [((Taps.)) | |

27	Juan:	*[de*	E/I VII

28	Gloria:	[((Is looking intently at the word on the board.))	R
29		[((Taps ruler under the "p" of *"personas."*))	
30		[(1.0)	

31	Juan:	*Yo no miro por sentar (xx)*	X
32		I can't see because of sitting (xx)	

33	Esteban:	*pers::*	I VIII

34	Gloria:	*[pers:sonal*	R
35		[((Taps twice.))	

36	Esteban:	*pers::sonas*	E/I IX

37	Juan:	*de personas*	E/I

38	Gloria:	*[pe son as::s*	R
39		[((Taps twice.))	

40	Juan:	*sonas*	E/I X

41	Gloria:	((Laughs.))	R

42	Juan:	*personas*	E

Something else besides Juan and Esteban's self-positioning as social subjects through agentive stances (by assisting Gloria) is happening in Example 14. The assistance technique employed most often by Juan and Esteban during this discourse sequence is that of "reading for." The "reading for" form of student-student assistance is interesting in that while it serves to position Juan and Esteban as active social subjects, it *may* be "objectifying" Gloria. The two men use this technique to provide assistance to Gloria with the reading of four words: (1) *esta* (Juan in line 5: "*esta*"); (2) *es* (Esteban in line 9: "*es*"); (3) *una* (Esteban in line 11, and Juan in line 12: "*una*"); and (4), *agrupación* (Esteban in line 18, and Juan in line 19: "*grupación*"). Whether this helps Gloria or not is not discernible from the data. In three of the four cases,[3] Gloria does not make a verbal attempt to read the words in question on her own before Juan and Esteban read the words for her. It may be that she truly needs the assistance, for before each "reading for" assistance

offered by Juan or Esteban, Gloria pauses for a discursively significant length of time, as if "stuck." She pauses in line 4 for 1.0
second, apparently not able to read the word *"esta."* She pauses
again in line 8, for 1.5 seconds, having trouble with the word *"es."*
And finally, she both pauses, in line 14 for 0.8 second and makes
a partially successful attempt at reading the word *"agrupación,"* in
lines 16-17—she is able to say *"°a::°."* In one case, however, Juan
and Esteban offer a "reading for" before Gloria has even had a
chance to pause and reflect. This occurs in lines 11-12, when they
read *"una"* for her. The frequency with which Juan and Esteban
offer Gloria "reading for" assistance, and especially the instance
in lines 11-12, when they read the word for Gloria before she is
even able to make her own attempt, "subjectifies" the two men,
but also "objectifies" Gloria. They have knowledge and will give it
to her rather than allowing her to build the knowledge with them.

This potentially unequal power relationship may come from
several sources. It could be that the two men are "doing-being"
hegemonic pedagogue, and acting out the role of teacher with
which they are most familiar, despite their two and a half months
with Daisy; teacher as knowledgeable "apostle" who gives the
word to students. Or, these actions could come from patriarchal
socialization. Under patriarchy, which is also part of the
hegemonic order in U.S. and Latin American societies—within and
outside of classrooms—men are the "knowers," "talkers" and
"doers." This translates into everyday discourse as men feeling
that they have the right to interrupt, speak over and/or speak for
women. Under this element of hegemony, from a Foucauldian perspective, men are seen by themselves, as well as by others who
have "disciplined" themselves to abide by it, as knowledgeable
authority figures whose right it is to interrupt, interject and take
the conversational "floor" when women are already in the process
of speaking. In this case, it could be for either or both of these reasons—or possibly for another reason altogether, like eagerness—
that Juan and Esteban are treating Gloria in this way. The potentially objectifying "reading for" technique is less frequently used
with the male than it is with the female students.

The discourse sequence in Example 14 was included because it
brings out this contradiction, and because it is representative of
other similar student actions.

Example 15
Juan, Esteban and Gloria Assist Fernando

During this brief discursive interchange, Fernando, arguably the most advanced literacy student in the classroom, is reading the sentence which ends, *"...proporcionarse crédito a intereses razonables"* ("...to offer credit at reasonable interest"). Juan, who received much support and assistance from Fernando and his other class-mates in Example 13, above, now assists *Fernando*, along with Esteban and Gloria, who is having trouble reading the words *"intereses"* and *"razonables."* Fernando begins this discourse se-quence by reading the words *"proporcionarse"* (line 1), *"crédito"* (line 3) and *"a"* (line 5)—in line 4, he mistakenly reads *"a"* as *"y."*

1	Fernando:	*pro por cionar se*	R
2		(0.2)	
3		*cré crédito*	
4		*y*	
5		*a̱ (.) a (.) a (.) °a°*	
6	Juan:	*i[n ter e̱s es*	I I
7	Esteban:	*[°in ter e°*	I
8	Fernando:	(0.4)	R
9		*a intereses*	
10	Esteban:	*°a°*	X
11	Fernando:	*ra zones*	R

The IRE sequences in this discourse sample are moderately open, and students continue to freely assume the roles of initia-tors, respondents and evaluators. The IRE configurations include an IIRR (I, above) and two E/I RE (II and III, below) sequences. These open IRE patterns, and the students' willingness to assume all roles within these patterns, indicate that discursive power dis-tribution in this classroom tends to remain more even under

Nadia—as it had under Daisy. As in the previous example, the teacher, Nadia, does not participate during Fernando's reading of the text.

12	Esteban:	*razonables*	E/I II
13	Fernando:	*ra ra [ra razonables*	R
14	Gloria:	*[ra zonables*	E

In this data sequence, students continue to position themselves as active social subjects through agentive stances, stances that place their knowledge and ability at the center of the learning process. Through these agentive stances, they continue to use a variety of assistance techniques in helping themselves and their peers read effectively. Here again, for example, Juan and Esteban use the "reading for" technique. In line 5, Fernando reads the word *"a"* from the sentence, *"...proporcionarse crédito a intereses razonables,"* but then he gets "stuck" and begins repeating *"a"* as he attempts to read *"intereses,"* the next word in the sentence: *"a̱ (.) a (.) a (.) °a°."* Juan and Esteban read it for him in lines 6 and 7. This appears to help Fernando. After a brief reflective pause (line 8), he reads *"intereses"* (line 9). Finally, Gloria offers assistance in the form of a "reading for" as Fernando is having trouble reading the word *"razonables"* in line 11. He produces the word *"razones"* ("reasons") instead of *"razonables"* ("reasonable"). Gloria uses the "reading for" technique again in line 14. Although this positions Gloria as an active social subject, it probably does not help Fernando, for he reads the word *"razonables"* correctly just as Gloria is offering her assistance (their utterances overlap, lines 13-14). This sequence concludes as follows:

15	Esteban:	*[razonables*	E/I III
16	Fernando:	*[razonables*	R
17		*(xx)*	
18	All:	((Give Fernando an applause.))	E

Another form of assistance offered to Fernando by his class-mates during this discourse sequence, and another way these students are assuming agentive stances, is the use of the "saying it correctly" technique. In line 11, again, Fernando is attempting to read the word *"razonables,"* but produces *"razones"* instead. The saying it correctly technique is employed by Esteban in line 12 when he reads the word for Fernando: *"razonables."* This effort is successful, and in line 13, Fernando attempts, and then succeeds, in reading *"razonables"*: *"ra ra ra razonables."* Even though Fernando has successfully read the word, Esteban uses the "saying it correctly" technique once more in line 15 (*"razonables"*). Fernando acknowledges Esteban by reading the word one more time (line 16), and then making a brief comment about his performance and their assistance (line 17).

This sequence ends with the students giving Fernando a round of applause. This action was coded as an agentive stance as well. By applauding, the students are acknowledging Fernando's accomplishment of reading the text. They could also be applauding the interactions that surrounded his reading of the text, that is, their successful co-construction of classroom knowledge. Nadia joins in the applause, smiles and laughs.

The Cundina: *Students Self-Position as Agents through Social Action*

Unfortunately, I was not able to collect interview data from Nadia's students before my field work ended in June of 1994,[4] as I had under Guillermo and Daisy. These interview data, which were collected toward the end of the tenure of both of these teachers, had proven valuable in at least partially gauging students' views and opinions on what their work with Guillermo and Daisy had meant for them. I was fortunate enough, however, to witness and document the birth of a social practice within their classroom which did seem to show that the students had internalized this growing view of agentive social self. This practice took the form of the *"cundina."*

The *cundina*[5] started as the *cooperativa* ("cooperative"). In early February of 1994, Nadia and her students were working on a unit around the generative theme of "community." When Nadia asked them for examples of "effective forms of community work, of solidarity," Esteban and Fernando brought up cooperatives. Nadia and her students then began discussing different forms of cooperatives, from child care and farming, to sewing and the production of basic products, to savings and lending cooperatives. The idea of a savings or lending cooperative was fresh in the students' minds, they said, because the month before an invited speaker had come to *Siempre* to address the students about their group's loans to *micro-empresas* ("micro-businesses"). Discussion of cooperatives within Nadia's classroom, however, soon turned to the more manageable idea of a *cundina*. Some students, depending on where in Latin America they were from, used the words "*tanda*" or "*amedia*" to describe a savings collective. The students, and Nadia, indicated that they were interested in forming either a savings and lending cooperative or a *cundina* as a way to improve their economic situations. On one cool evening in mid-February, Fernando said, "Let's organize one and do the work!" And thus the idea was born.

In late February, the class held an official meeting with Daisy—who was now working only as the program co-coordinator and not as a teacher—to propose their idea for a savings and lending cooperative. Daisy took the group's ideas to her superior at *Siempre*, Federico, and organized a meeting so that the students could present their ideas to him. The students and Nadia again made their presentation, this time to Federico. While supportive, Daisy and Federico listed concerns they had that would be important to address before going forward: What exact kind of financial cooperative did the class want to form? Savings? Lending? Both? To whom would they lend? Where would they keep their money? Would they work with a bank? Would they have a physical location? How would they raise capital?

Over the next two months, as the class considered these and other logistical questions, they studied the theme of "*cooperativa*" in their classroom—the three data sequences in this chapter are all drawn from a lesson that was part of this thematic unit. In mid-April, Nadia and her students decided that, due to time, financial and other limitations, a cooperative might not be the best thing for them. But they still wanted to collaborate on some sort of financial activity that would benefit them all. So they decided, instead of a cooperative, to form a *cundina*. Fernando, Esteban, Nadia, three students from two other classrooms and myself formed our *cundina* by putting our names, in numbered order, on a piece of paper, and then contributing twenty dollars each. Every member of the *cundina* would contribute twenty dollars per week, and the "pot" of one hundred seventy dollars would be given to the next person on the list until everyone had received it once. At the end of this cycle, members could leave the *cundina*, and newcomers could join. The *cundina* continued and grew in membership past the time my field work ended at *Siempre*. It became, in fact, quite popular.

This group of poor, working class, formerly illiterate, largely undocumented immigrant students, who had only months earlier felt as if "from us comes nothing," now saw themselves as active social subjects who were capable of researching, studying about and putting into place a financial organization that might take the form of a complex savings and lending cooperative. Although the group eventually abandoned the idea of the cooperative because they felt they were not getting the support they needed from *Siempre*, nor that they had the time that would be necessary to do all that was needed to form the institution, they carried through with the formation of a *cundia*. By forming, maintaining, and enlarging the *cundina* over time, these students were taking a concrete action on a problematic socio/political/economic situation in their lives. They were trying to find a way to save money without having to open a costly bank account. Opening up such an account might require a minimum balance, charge fees or require that they provide forms of documentation and identification they did not possess. They got around these hurdles, and solved their problems, by counting on themselves and each other, by taking action on their world in order to change it. Forming a *cundina* represents a social self-positioning on the part of the students that is agentive.

Understanding Nadia's Classroom

As elaborated in the discourse sequences and cooperative/*cundina* descriptions presented in the examples above, it was the students who recognized and solved many of their own reading, writing and social problems, and who created a safe and comfortable environment in which to do this. The learning environment—the pedagogic discourse community—that was constructed by the students was one where power relations were more evenly distributed between the students and their teacher than has been characteristic of both traditional, teacher-centered adult literacy programs in general (Kozol 1985) and of this very same classroom and students under Guillermo. Perhaps as an act of resistance to the program, Nadia ironically provided the *space* for the students to co-construct a counter-hegemonic discourse community that challenged the notion of students as disempowered empty vessels.

Students would also occasionally help each other during reading under Guillermo, but they were generally not encouraged to do so. When students interjected while their classmates read, it was usually to read "over" them. They would rarely try to assist each other as was observed under Nadia. They began doing this under Daisy, as she encouraged them to draw on themselves as legitimate providers of academic knowledge. When Daisy says, in Example 9, "You're right. Next time, I'll correct it" (line 11); "Very good. I was thinking '*cajeta*,' a sweet. But very good. That's good" (lines 13-14); and "What's your opinion?" (line 17), or "Like Ignacio said, the only way to know them is to read them" (lines 14-15); and "Let me sum-up what you said, Ignacio. And tell me if I'm wrong" (lines 20-21), in Example 10, above, she is socializing students through language to see themselves as potential active social subjects. And although there appears to be some backing away from the kinds of student-centered classroom activities Daisy encouraged among the students—lengthy socio-political discussions, the student generation of text and original writing versus copying—these lessons, these new views of self as legitimate social agents, seem to have held, and grown, under Nadia.

While Nadia is a traditional, teacher-centered pedagogue with the same philosophical orientation as Guillermo, her classroom actions—or *in*actions—allowed for the establishment of a different discourse community than had existed under either Guillermo or Daisy. While continuing to embrace the traditional teacher-centered exercises they expressed a preference for, and that Nadia provided for them, the students *also* continued to assume agentive stances and to situate themselves and their classmates as active social subjects.

Nadia would "objectify" her students in the sense that she selected almost all of the themes, texts and activities herself that they would work on and expect her students to engage that content and those activities. And the students seemed to accept this. But during actual discursive classroom interaction, Nadia would not only refrain from either objectifying *or* subjectifying the students, but she would refrain, for the most part, from participation altogether. Through the students' active assumption of agentive stances, their subjectification of one another, and through Nadia's "turning-over" of much of the classroom discourse management, the students successfully and repeatedly collaborated in the formation of a discourse community that was counter-hegemonic; a discourse community that challenged the notion of student as disempowered, empty vessel. In juxtaposition to the social practices in Guillermo's classroom, Nadia appeared to be an accomplice with her students in the formation of a classroom with "critical substance" but little "critical vocabulary."

This chapter presented findings and discussion on the forms of social practice that fostered the development of student agency in the classroom of Nadia Monterey and her students. Through a presentation of representative examples from the data, it was demonstrated how the individuals in this classroom collectively produced a learning community that was comprised of both "hegemonic" and "counter-hegemonic" elements, but how, in the end, this community was dominated by counter-hegemonic practices that positioned and produced students as critical agents.

The final chapter, "Implications for Real Life," will go back and re-explore some of the problems I raised at the beginning of this book—now in light of the findings and discussion presented in this and the two previous chapters. What questions have I answered? What have I not answered? What remains to further explore...?

Notes

1. There were a number of errors in the Spanish text that Nadia had written on the board. Those errors have been reproduced here—to the best of my and Microsoft Word's ability. They include the inappropriate use of the upper case "T," the lack of capitalization where necessary, the lack of consistency in the use of accents, the use of the letter "u" instead of "v," and the use of a combination upper and lower case "j" that appears as an upper case "J" with a dot over it.

2. This written text was produced in Spanish. I have included an

English translation below each original Spanish text for the reader. English translation will also be included in the discursive sequences used in all the examples below, where possible and appropriate. The sequences themselves are being presented in their original Spanish because the nature of the talk deals directly with how the students and teacher are reading the Spanish language, word by word.

3. She does try to read *"esta"* (line 1) before Juan reads it for her in line 5.

4. This was a traumatic and change-filled month for the students of *Siempre's Alfa 2* class. I, who had become a regular fixture and friend to many students, left to intensify and finish my data reduction and analysis. Daisy left to pursue other work and graduate studies. And their third teacher, Nadia, also left. She went on to find a better paying job with daytime hours so that she could take evening ESL classes.

5. A *cundina*, a term Nadia and her students said is used in El Salvador, is a savings collective. A *cundina* is used to describe a group of people who come together to make weekly contributions to a group "pot." Each week, the collected money goes to a different member of the group. *Cundina* comes from the Spanish verb *cundinar*, which translates, "to spread, propagate, multiply."

References

Kozol, J. 1985. *Illiterate America*. New York: Plume Press.

Rogoff, B. 1990. *Apprenticeship in Thinking*. New York: Oxford University Press.

_____ . 1991. "Social Interaction as Apprenticeship in Thinking: Guided Participation in Spatial Planning." In Resnick, L., Levine, J. and Teasley, S., eds., *Perspectives on Socially Shared Cognition*. Washington, D.C.: American Psychological Association.

Implications for Real Life: Critical Pedagogy and Student Agency

Prohibieron ir a la escuela,
e ir a la universidad.
Prohibieron las garantias,
y el fin constitucional.
Prohibieron todas las ciencias,
excepto la militar.
Prohibieron el derecho a queja,
prohibieron el preguntar.
Hoy te sugiero, mi hermano,
pa' que no vuelva a pasar,
¡Prohibido olvidar!

—Rubén Blades ("Prohibido Olvidar")[1]

After spending every Thursday evening for over a year in the heart of L.A.'s Central American community with Guillermo, Daisy, Nadia and their Spanish literacy students, and after having spent an equal amount of time organizing, reducing, analyzing and "living with"[2] the data I was fortunate enough to collect—thanks to the generosity, openness and desire for self-improvement of the participants in this community-based educational project—I gained fresh insight, and began to more fully understand, first hand, something critical social scientists already know (and positivistic scientists are secretly afraid to admit): We create our own social, pedagogical, racial, cultural, gendered and political discursive realities; we re-produce our own hegemonies.

Sure, the fifteen-year-old Indonesian who looses a finger working the stitching machine at the Nike plant because she is wracked with fatigue at the end of her eighteen hour shift—and who is afraid to speak-out or join the union for fear of government/death squad/CIA reprisals—is suffering under a semi-post-neo-meta-narrative not quite of her own making. This archetypal victim of global capital expansion, this woman living in a "sweat shop Suzy"/Kathy Lee Gifford nightmare is not so different from Pete Wilson's dreaded "job stealing" Chicano field worker picking *tomates* in California's central valley, or the African American grandmother who cleans others' houses in the diaspora of Chicago's wealthy European American suburbs. They are part of the oppressed Freire began to centralize in the radical educational literature thirty years ago. They suffer because racism, imperialism, class exploitation and sexism are quite "real"—at least in the sense that the victims of these phenomena feel their effects very personally. However, although they did not necessarily create these conditions directly themselves, they *do* participate in the production and maintenance of these conditions.

Could the factory workers in Madonna's *homage* to the proletarian in all of us, "Express Yourself," storm the boss' living quarters at the top of the stairs and seize the means of production? Yes. Could the Reagan-era air traffic controllers have formed a militant anarcho-syndicalist[3] union and called all public sector workers to a general strike against the anti-worker slash-and-burn tactics that Ron began and now Bill is continuing? Yes. Could "mild-mannered" school teachers become radicalized, realize their full potential as "organic" (Gramsci 1971), "transformative" (Giroux 1988) and "committed" (McLaren, Fischman, Serra & Antelo, 1988) intellectuals at the forefront of a struggle for social justice in North America? Yes. Are these scenarios likely—at least in the near future? Probably not. And why? Because of hegemony. This is not the way things are done.

"Sure," most North Americans say (including the Chicano *Californiano*, African American grandmother and "professional" public school teacher), "There's lots of room for improvement. Our system's not perfect. But you don't just storm the palace gates. You go to school. You listen to and watch the news. You vote." Those who talk this talk have become self-policing. Outrageous systems of oppression have become normalized. Hegemony reigns supreme. So, are these folks the victims of cigar smoking wealthy White men sitting in board rooms in Manhattan, Paris, London and Sydney? Yes. But are they also complicit in their own oppression? Yes. Could they also be complicit in their own liberation? Definitely.

This is what happened—although in very subtle, small and quiet ways (and I agree with Daisy when she said, "Sometimes actions are small, step-by-step...to have[/find] a voice, this is political. To me, this is transformational")—in the classrooms of Daisy and Nadia, in the store-front leased by *Siempre Adelante*, which shared the parking lot with the *pupusería*, video store and beauty parlor off Foxbourne Boulevard; such was the case for Esteban, Farabundo, Ignacio, Ana, Gloria, Veronica, Juan, Samuel and Fernando. These students created an alternative pedagogic, counter-hegemonic space for themselves. They carved it out of the classroom discourse by eventually assuming resistant and agentive stances in relation to traditional and dis-empowering ways of teaching and learning.

This was not accomplished in a vacuum. "Committed intellectual" Daisy began subjectifing students by treating them as active social subjects. And "semi-banking educator" Nadia, through her non-obstructivist bowing-out of the process, in essence, also continued to subjectify students. So despite Guillermo's objectification of students, and the students' assumption of conformist and resistant stances—producing a hegemonic discourse community earlier in their educational process at *Siempre*—the students, with Daisy and Nadia, were later able to create counter-hegemonic discourse communities in their classrooms which fostered the development of critical student agency.

But what are some of the larger implications of these findings? How do these findings impact critical pedagogical theory, research and practice? What do they mean for the continuing debate on agency? In the remainder of this chapter, these and other similar larger issues will be considered in light of the findings. First, issues of "critical language" versus "critical practice" will be discussed. Second, the relative importance of the role of the teacher versus role of the student in the creation of critical classroom practices will be raised. Third, the differential development of academic and sociopolitical critical student agency that was evidenced in the study will be highlighted and problematized. Fourth, the issue of gender relations, the role they play in classroom power relations, and what effect this has on the development of critical student agency, will be discussed. Fifth, a potential alternative explanation for the critical student agency that developed will be raised. Sixth, how these issues could be raised in future research agenda will be elaborated. Seventh, and finally, the impact these findings have on the field of critical pedagogy will be discussed.

Beyond a "Critical Vocabulary"

One issue that became clear in my analysis of the data from Guillermo's classroom is that employing the language, the vocabulary, of Freirean pedagogy alone was not enough, in-and-of-itself, to foster critical student agency. This use of "critical vocabulary" emerged from the data as an approach consistently employed by Guillermo. At teacher training session he would agree with the need to bring "critical consciousness" to students. During lessons he would focus on politically-oriented themes that were relevant to his students. Yet the hegemonic pedagogical practices that he embraced in his classroom appeared to undercut whatever positive effect his use of sociopolitical themes, and Freirean language, might have had.

Based on the data from the other two classrooms, it became clear that the social and discursive relationships *themselves* needed to actively promote counter-hegemonic practices for the Freirean/critical approach to be even remotely effective in relation to its stated objectives. Students must be allowed, and encouraged, to take agentive stances that locate them as active social subjects within learning situations. If classroom social relations, at the discursive level, are not transformed so as to encourage this type of development within students, then generative themes, political issues or lip service to "conscientization" will not successfully promote the development of critical student agency. Careful attention must be paid to the day-to-day talk, actions and interactions *within* Freirean-minded classrooms to foster critical student agency and consciousness.

Parts of a Whole:
Teachers and Students in Critical Social Practice

Whose actions are most important in this process of developing critical student agency? The teacher's or students'? Many social theorists posit the centrality of the teacher in processes of social change. Gramsci (1971), for example, views teachers, among others, as potential "organic intellectuals" who, through the construction and promotion of a counter-hegemonic vision and culture, can help bring about social and economic change to better society. Within the critical educational literature there is also a focus on the important role played by the teacher, who is seen as a driving, authoritative force behind student empowerment (Freire 1970). Giroux, for example, envisions teachers as "transformative intellectuals" and "cultural workers" (1992) who can help to foster social transformation from within schools and other cultural sites. Fischman and McLaren, in redefining Gramsci's notion of the organic intellectual, refer to teachers as potential *"committed* intellectuals" (Fischman 1998; McLaren, Fischman, Serra & Antelo 1988; emphasis mine) who can play key roles in schools and classrooms in agitating for social change and justice.

Given these theories, is it the actions of students in conforming, resisting or acting agentively that fosters student agency? Or is it the actions of teachers in positioning students as passive or active social subjects that is the determining factor? The empirical data from this study seem to show, in a critical context, what we already know from the sociocultural (Gutierrez 1992, 1993, 1994; Lave & Wenger 1991; Ochs 1988, 1993; Rogoff 1990, 1991), Foucauldian (1977a) and poststructuralist (Laclau & Mouffe 1985; Lyotard 1989) literature. Social practices, within or outside of classrooms, oppressive or transformative, are *always* co-constructions. So it was as well in this study, where a combination of the social positions teachers placed their students in, *and* the positions the students themselves allowed, or did not allow, themselves to fill, determined whether or not hegemonic pedagogical practices were embraced or challenged, and whether a hegemonic *or* counter-hegemonic discourse community developed.

Academic and Sociopolitical Forms of Critical Student Agency

Analyses of the data also indicated that learners developed significant levels of "academic" critical student agency under both Daisy and Nadia. These students began to regularly assume central roles in the construction and dissemination of classroom knowledge. They began, and then continued, to see themselves as legitimate and active social actors in their classrooms, actors who had something significant to contribute. The students began to read the "word" through their readings of the "world" (Freire & Macedo 1987). The analyses also showed that students had begun to develop "sociopolitical" critical agency with Daisy and Nadia, although on a much more limited scale than their development of academic critical student agency. Under Daisy, Gloria became active on the Student Council, and Veronica attended her first political march and rally in Los Angeles. Under Nadia, the students formed the *cundina*. Through their suggestion, creation and expansion of this financial collective, as well as through their investigations into the more ambitious idea of a savings and lending cooperative, Nadia's students demonstrated sociopolitical agency.

These actions were significant for the students. For many of them, these sociopolitical acts represented their first foray into political activism in the daunting megalopolis of Los Angeles. These students began to *re*-read the world through their *re*-reading of the word. Yet these activities on the Council, at the march and rally, and through the *cundia* represented the extent of sociopolitical agentive stances I was able to observe beyond the academic sphere. That is to say, these kinds of sociopolitical activities, and agentive stances, were relatively rare for Guillermo, Daisy and Nadia's students. And sociopolitical stances and actions on a grander, more politically aggressive and militant scale, as described in the Freirean and critical literature—such as the organization of unions, strikes, political/informational campaigns, picketing or forming alternative governmental institutions (Adams 1975; Arnove & Dewees 1991; Freire & Horton 1990; Freire & Macedo 1987; Hirshon & Butler 1983; La Belle 1986; Solorzano 1989; Torres 1991)—did not occur for the students is this classroom at all.

As the data from this study indicate, the development of academic critical student agency may have helped students read the word of the literacy classroom in an empowering way, but did it help them *significantly* read and re-read (or re-write) their worlds outside of the classroom? I have come to agree with Daisy, when she said that for her, small changes, within the classroom context—often occurring just within individuals—are transformational. Large scale political activism is not the only way to bring about substantive changes in people's lives. If only a few students in each of *Siempre's* classes began to see themselves as potential social and political agents—through their transformed *academic* roles within classrooms—then the Freirean pedagogical endeavor would have been worthwhile. This is not a replacement for revolution, but it *can be* revolutionary.

What Role Gender?

During analyses of the data, a question arose that I had not anticipated (although maybe I should have): What role did gender power relations play in fostering or hindering the development of critical student agency among this group of learners? While this question was not the specific focus of the study, and cannot be definitively answered here, it gives me cause to reflect. As I began data collection at *Siempre*, I was surprised, demographically, by the large numbers of women students in attendance. Forty three percent of all students in *Siempre's* ESL and literacy classes were women. Studies have shown that while women are *over*-represented among illiterates, they are often *under*-represented in literacy classes (Kozol 1985; Weiler 1988). Some researchers claim this is due, in part, to the fact that illiterate women are prevented from attending literacy programs by their husbands, boyfriends and fathers for the purposes of social and political control (Kozol 1985; Rockhill 1987; Weiler 1988). For this reason, I did not expect to encounter as many women as I did studying Spanish and English literacy within *Siempre's* classrooms.

Not only were there many women present within the institution, but my formal observations and data analyses of Guillermo, Daisy and Nadia's classrooms (as well as intermittent observations of two other teachers' classrooms), revealed that these women were active classroom participants. Under Guillermo, Daisy and Nadia, the female students were active in thirty-nine percent of the discursive "turns" (initiating, responding or evaluating) in which students participated. Further, the women were equally distributed by ability. For example, Ana and Veronica were among the intermediate Spanish literacy class' most advanced students, and Benita, Gloria, and a woman named Teodora, were among the group's least advanced students. And finally, the female students were even more active than the male students in the area of student governance, with sixty percent of the Student Council being composed of women.

Yet a numeric analysis of the data also revealed that when the female students under Nadia were offered assistance, this assistance took the form of "reading for" thirty-four percent of the time, while in only thirteen percent of the cases was this technique used with male students. As noted in the discussion in Chapter 6, the use of "reading for" can run the risk of positioning the recipient of the assistance as a "passive social subject," even while it is simultaneously positioning the student *offering* the assistance as an "active social subject." This is especially the case if the student attempting to read is given little time to read the text in question before the assistance provider reads it for them. This situation is even more complicated when it is a male student who is reading the word for a female student, as questions of patriarchy and hegemonic pedagogical practices arise. It would be wise for future similar research to consider the role of gender in the development of critical student agency.

Critical Agentive Growth:
Product of Critical Social Practices or Just "Learning"?

What else could have caused this gradual shift toward critical student agency among these students? That is, could the students' development of critical agency have been caused by other than how teachers socially positioned them, or how they socially positioned themselves, through discourse? The answer is yes, there *could have* been a number of other factors that aided in the development of critical student agency, especially on the academic plane. One of the most plausible alternative explanations could be that of the natural chronological learning curve. It has been suggested to me that the students in this study might have begun to act more agentively under Nadia not only because they had been socialized to see themselves as legitimate academic and social agents, but because they had simply developed higher Spanish literacy skill over time, and that this began to manifest itself under their third teacher. It is very possible that this played a part in the students' agentive development over the year of the study. This study did not include, however, pre- and post-literacy tests delivered at the beginning and end of data collection—or at the beginning and end of each teacher's tenure. Beyond the potential methodological dissonance this might have personally and philosophically caused, the focus of this study, instead, was always on the implementation of Freirean practice; specifically, the development of critical student agency, and not literacy development, *per se*.

But it is possible that growing academic competence on the students' part—after having studied, albeit, with three unique and very different teachers—*did* play a role in their growing confidence in assuming agentive academic stances in the classroom. Yet analyses of the data seems to indicate that this was not the *primary* factor in students' agentive development. The problem with this potential competing hypothesis is the following. The more advanced students could have, for example, simply acted as a hegemonic teacher might act, displaying their academic superiority by consistently giving answers to their less academically advanced classmates. This would have been coded as agentive for these students. But the critical agency displayed by the more academically advanced students more often took another form. It took a form, yes, where they could demonstrate their abilities, but also where they could assist and apprentice their less advanced classmates. It was through these acts that the more advanced students both assumed agentive stances for themselves, *and* positioned their less advanced classmates as active social subjects at the same time. While simply giving answers—"reading for"—did occur thirty-four percent of the time for female students, and fourteen percent of the time for male students, seventy-six percent of the time (averaged between the men and women), more academically advanced students would use their skills in ways to *help* their classmates in their reading instead of just reading for them. Therefore, if natural academic growth accounted for the increase in academic critical student agency, why were more advanced students' agentive stances put to the task of assisting less advanced students at the time? This is an important issue that will need to be more centrally considered and accounted for in future research

Future Criticalist Research

Future research in this area will need to continue to explore the social and discursive development of critical student agency, but with some variations. First, we should attempt similar investigations at diverse sites and in different contexts: from elementary to secondary schools, in classes working in English as well as Spanish, within and outside of the United States, in formal and informal learning settings, in classes comprised of predominantly women or predominately men, and in classrooms self-identified as "critical" or "Freirean" in orientation, as well as in classrooms *not* so identified. Would my findings from *Siempre Adelante's Alfa 2* class hold across contexts? If so, how? If not, why? It would be interesting, for example, to see if one could find instances of critical student agency, as I have defined it in this study, emerging in classrooms that are specifically *not* self-defined as "Freirean," and then try to explain the differences and causes.

Besides these changes in venue and context, I would suggest other changes, some subtle, some more substantive, in a study of this nature, that would assist us as criticalists in answering some of the questions raised in the discussion above. These changes would center around embracing a more participatory, action-oriented research paradigm that would allow participants to include their concerns, and voice the outcomes they would like to see, as part of the research project. Such an approach to research would go beyond simply "studying" teachers and their students, and should actually assist them in implementing critical and transformative strategies in their own classrooms, turning them from the "subjected" who are studied from afar, to "historical subjects" capable of transforming their own lived realities as they see them. This study was not, for reasons within and outside of my personal control, grounded within such a "participatory action research" framework, although I wish it had been.

Critical Pedagogical Theory, Research and Teaching

In this study, I attempted to bridge critical pedagogical theory and practice by examining discursive social practices in one self-defined Freirean/critical classroom. One of my goals was to address the problem that most of the Freirean literature does not provide empirical examples, or data from classrooms, of how critical student agency is or is not successfully constructed between students and teachers. While most Freirean literature and research focuses on large scale societal, school-wide or classroom-wide change and agentive growth in students, this study attempted to demonstrate how change occurred, over time, among individual students at the level of discourse—within daily, regularized talk and interaction. Additionally, in this study, empirical data from an actual classroom was used, as opposed to focusing solely on general demographic and political outcomes. It is my hope that for these reasons, this study has positively contributed to the Freirean literature.

On the level of theory, the findings presented and the questions raised by this study might be able to serve both to extend the debate on human agency among criticalist thinkers in education, and also to provide a bridge between social theorizing on agency, and what is being practiced in schools and other settings. The focus on the specific discursive formation of critical student agency has raised both a challenge, and offered an example, to researchers working in the field of critical pedagogy. It is a challenge in that few studies within critical pedagogy have attempted to explicitly examine the how students develop critical agency at the level of micro-discursive talk or that use empirical data from classrooms. At the same time, it might offer an example as to one way to envision and organize such research.

Finally, these findings and questions might also prove useful to critical practitioners. Through understanding what aided in the development of critical student agency among Guillermo, Daisy and Nadia's students, critical teachers might examine their own practices, especially at the level of their day-to-day and regularized discourse patterns, to see if they are possibly unwittingly maintaining hegemonic relationships despite what they feel is Freirean and liberatory.

Above all, we must remember that the struggle for social justice in not an easy or quick one. As *compañero* Freire wrote in *Pedagogy of the Oppressed* (1970:31):

Freedom is acquired by conquest, not by gift.

Notes

1. I would like to thank and give credit to Rubén Blades, author and performer, and Rubén Blades Publishing, publisher and copyright holder, for the use of an excerpt from Rubén's inspiring song, "Prohibido Olvidar." Plus, it's got a good beat and you can dance to it...

2. Something every good doctoral student and researcher steeped in the ethnographic tradition is, or should be, familiar with.

3. For more on anarcho-sydicalism, see Noam Chomsky's *Notes on Anarchism* (1994); Daniel Guérin's *Anarchism* (1970); and Rudolf Rocker's *Anarcho-syndicalism* (1938).

References

Adams, F. 1975. *Unearthing Seeds of Fire*. Winston-Salem: John F. Blair.

Arnove, R. and Dewees, A. 1991. "Education and Revolution in Nicaragua, 1979-1990." *Comparative Education Review* 35: 92-109.

Chomsky, N. 1994. *Notes on Anarchism*. Grand Rapids: Discussion Bulletin.

Fischman, G. 1998. "Donkeys and Superteachers: Structural Adjustment and Popular Education in Latin America." *International Review of Education* 42: 177-199.

Foucault, M. 1977a. *Discipline and Punish: The Birth of the Prison*. Sheridan, A., trans. New York: Pantheon.

Freire, P. 1970. *Pedagogy of the Oppressed*. Rámos, M., trans. New York: Continuum.

Freire, P. & Horton, M. 1990. *We Make the Road By Walking: Conversations on Education and Social Change*. Bell, B., Gaventa, J., and Peters, J., eds. Philadelphia: Temple University Press.

Freire, P. & Macedo, D. 1987. *Literacy: Reading the Word and the World*. Massachusetts: Bergin & Garvey.

Giroux, H. 1988. *Teachers as Intellectuals: Toward a Critical Pedagogy of Learning*. Westport: Bergin & Garvey.

_____ . 1992. *Border Crossings: Cultural Workers and the Politics of Education*. New York: Routledge.

Gramsci. A. 1971. *Selections from the Prison Notebooks*. Medea, Q. and Smith, N., eds. and trans. London: Lawrence & Wishart.

Guérin, D. 1970. *Anarchism*. New York: Monthly Review Press.

Gutierrez, K. 1992. "A Comparison of Instructional Contexts in Writing Process Classrooms with Latino Children." *Education and Urban Society* 24: 244-262.

_____ . 1993. "Scripts, Counterscripts and Multiple Scripts." Paper presented at the annual meeting of the American Educational Research Association. Atlanta, Georgia.

_____ . 1994. "How Talk, Context, and Script Shape Contexts for Learning: A Cross-Case Comparison of Journal Sharing." *Linguistics and Education* 5: 335-365.

Hirshon, S. and Butler, J. 1983. *And Also Teach Them to Read*. Westport: Lawerence Hill.

Kozol, J. 1985. *Illiterate America*. New York: Plume Press.

La Belle, T. J. 1986. *Non-Formal Education in Latin America and the Caribbean: Stability, Reform, or Revolution?* New York: Praeger.

Laclau, E. and Mouffe, C. 1985. *Hegemony and Socialist Strategy: Towards a Radical Democratic Politics*. London: Verso.

Lave, J. and Wenger, E. 1991. *Situated Learning: Legitimate Peripheral Participation*. Cambridge: Cambridge University Press.

Lyotard, J. 1989. *The Lyotard Reader*. Benjamin, A., ed. London: Basil Blackwell.

McLaren, P., Fischman, G., Serra, S. and Antelo, E. 1988. "The Specters of Gramsci: Revolutionary Praxis and the Committed Intellectual." *Journal of Thought*.

Ochs, E. 1988. *Culture and Language Development*. Cambridge: Cambridge University Press.

_____ . 1993. "Constructing Social Identity: A Language Socialization Perspective." *Research on Language and Social Interaction* 26: 287-306.

Rocker, R. 1938. *Anarcho-syndicalism*. London.

Rockhill, K. 1987. "Gender, Language and the Politics of Literacy." *British Journal of Sociology of Education* 8: 153-167.

Rogoff, B. 1990. *Apprenticeship in Thinking*. New York: Oxford University Press.

_____ . 1991. "Social Interaction as Apprenticeship in Thinking: Guided Participation in Spatial Planning." In Resnick, L., Levine, J. and Teasley, S., eds., *Perspectives on Socially Shared Cognition*. Washington, D.C.: American Psychological Association.

Solorzano, D. 1989. "Teaching Social Change: Reflections on a Freirean Approach in a College Classroom." *Teaching Sociology* 17: 218-225.

Torres, C. A. 1991. "The State, Non-Formal Education, and Socialism in Cuba, Nicaragua, and Grenada." *Comparative Education Review* 35: 110-130.

Weiler, K. 1988. *Women Teaching for Change: Gender, Class and Power*. South Hadley: Bergin & Garvey.

Afterword

[Teachers] should aspire...to shorten more and more the distance between what they say and what they do.

—Paulo Freire (*Pedagogy of the Heart*)

Upon reading *Discourse Wars in Gotham-West*, I was filled with childhood memories of my family's struggle to survive their migration from Puerto Rico to Los Angeles in the 1950s and the alienation we faced, particularly within the context of public schools. These are the sort of persisting memories that constantly interact—today's representations of reality intermingling interminably with the past. And nowhere is this more true than in the lives of working class Latino immigrant families who have had to leave behind the recognizable intonations of their native language, the distinguishable landscapes of their homeland, and the physical resonance of a way of life that was familiar and comforting, even in light of the great economic and political difficulties they may have faced. Yet unfortunately, the tremendous impact of this personal dimension of the immigrant experience seems so thoughtlessly ignored or denied within the context of traditional classroom pedagogy.

Similar to my family's experience, the new life that Latino immigrants find in the U.S. is too often filled with disappointment and frustration, particularly when they must confront the false illusions of U.S. prosperity fueled back home by the insipid globalized images of the media—powerful images that, too often, both homogenize and distort the aspirations, desires and dreams of Latino immigrants who long for a better life. Instead of safety and security, what many immigrants are quickly forced to confront are the racialized institutional policies and practices that give rise to painful flashbacks of injustice and impunity— conditions they thought had been left behind in their war-torn or economically distressed countries.

Over the past century, intense debates have raged regarding the impact of poor and working class immigrants on the economy and the labor market, particularly if their incorporation was devoid of U.S. political interests. Nowhere has the impact of anti-immigrant sentiments and the economic consequences of globalization been more felt than by Latino immigrant residents of Los Angeles. More recently, the politics of the INS and "public" initiatives (such as Proposition 187 and 227) that call for the passage of anti-immigrant legislation in California, have severely functioned to curtail the social agency of Latino immigrant populations—many of whom find themselves within these borders solely as a consequence of the deleterious effects of U.S. foreign economic policies in Latin America. Through glamorized images of wealth and democracy, the U.S. openly invites Latin American populations to both idealize and consume *American*. It is only when they arrive here that the *open* invitation is retracted, at least to the disenfranchised. So, while folks are unconscionably seduced to put on the veneer of American life *in their own country*, to seek a life in America, or Gotham-West, is another story.

Marc Pruyn's engaging study painstakingly has sought to understand what happens to Latino immigrant students who, while struggling to survive within the realities of a rapidly changing political economy in Los Angeles, have worked to develop the literacy skills that might mean the difference between life-long menial labor and *un trababjo decente* (a decent job), as my mother would say when she was struggling to liberate herself from the wretched conditions of the sweatshops on Santee Street. What is most heartening about Pruyn's work is the respect, faith, and love for the people that ground his endeavors to carefully study the process by which students within a Freirean-oriented adult literacy program come to develop their ability to act in socially and politically transformative ways—knowledge that perhaps might also guide our efforts to support transformative social movements among Latino immigrant populations within a larger context.

Unlike the work of most critical theorists, Pruyn enhances his nine years of critical teaching experience with thirteen months of classroom empirical observations to engage forthrightly the important question of critical practice. His analysis of micro-interactional levels of discourse, and what it reveals, challenges us, as teachers, to rethink our traditional concepts of good critical practice. Never has the notion that "we might be politically correct

and pedagogically all wrong" been more evident or better illus-
trated than in the results of Pruyn's study. Intentionally (or unin-
tentionally), his work brings to light the too rarely discussed
problematic of over-zealous politicized discourses, which might
represent an accurate analysis of truth, but that in the constant
telling and retelling can rob students of the critical space necessary
for an authentic process of *conscientizacao* to take place. I am particularly struck by this dimension of Pruyn's study, since I too, no
doubt, have been unwittingly guilty of this error. Like Guillermo,
there are times when I have certainly spoken too quickly or been
too eager to get my students moving toward a *liberatory* path of an
issue or a theme, rather than to allow them the space to struggle
individually and collectively with greater intellectual freedom. In
the process of such reflection and self-critic, we as educators must
ultimately engage the manner in which power operates within the
context of our classrooms.

In many ways, Pruyn's study is truly groundbreaking, for he is
one of the first to empirically suggest that if provided the critical
space, students are more likely to break out of the classroom pas-
sivity that can incarcerate their consciousness and creativity, than
if they are too quickly "guided" toward a particular critical ideological direction by the teacher. There is no question in my mind
that Pruyn's work challenges critical educators to rethink the nature of student discourses and thus, how we use teacher authority
to create the conditions for democratic classroom life. For Pruyn,
critical student agency cannot be divorced from the contextual realities that inform its production, *both outside and within the classroom*. And more importantly, the development of critical student
agency cannot be postponed until students learn the vocabulary or
their writing ability improves. Instead, he makes the case that it
must be embodied within a revolutionary process that is fundamentally rooted in the least expected moments of *la vida cotidiana*
and the very ordinariness of everyday life.

Amidst our constant struggles to be good critical educators,
Pruyn's work also reminds us that critical pedagogy is a process
and relationship that matures over time, as much for the students
as the teacher. Here, I return to the student-teacher/teacher-
student dialectic that Freire so often discussed in his work. From
this perspective, both teachers and students require the critical

space to learn and to expand their consciousness and sense of critical social agency—and for many, this process may first begin through responses of resistance. As such, we must come to understand with greater depth and specificity how student and teacher resistance can often be linked to experiences of loss or invasion of the necessary critical space required for reflection and learning—an interpretation that might help us to consider, more effectively and in a new light, acts of student and teacher resistance in our own work.

Given such an interpretation, Nadia's classroom—the co-creation of one teacher's resistance and her students' responses—renders greater meaning to the notion of classroom co-construction and the significance of social positioning of both teachers and the students within the process of schooling. By the same token, it cannot be overlooked that the pedagogical maturity of the students over the year, as a consequence of the critical pedagogical interactions experienced in Daisy's class, was also essential to both teacher and student social positioning and the expression of critical agency they later displayed in Nadia's classroom.

Yet, the question still remains: How do we, in our political commitment to uproot the hegemonic educational practices that support capitalist domination and exploitation, participate in the co-creation of classroom discourses that both support critical space and yet, forthrightly challenge the ideological structures of economic inequality and racism? What is undeniable in Pruyn's work is the absence of a particular *formula* to solve the *discourse wars* so prevalent in the classroom experience of Latino immigrant students today. Instead, he contends that in the midst of our liberatory pedagogical efforts we must return often to two formidable insights drawn from Gramsci's work. The first encompasses the notion that critical pedagogical co-creation must be organically linked to material relations of power. And the second is that we will consistently need to struggle with the conflicts and contradictions associated with deeply internalized hegemonic structures—structures that give rise to both responses of resistance and critical social agency in our classrooms. More simply put, *Discourse Wars in Gotham-West* challenges us anew, in the tradition of Paulo Freire, to struggle daily "to shorten more and more the distance between what we say and what we do" in our relationships with our students, our colleagues, and the communities in which we work, live, and dream.

Antonia Darder,
Claremont Graduate University

Appendices

Appendix A

The transcription conventions used in the organization of the data examples presented in this study have been adapted from Atkinson & Heritage (1984) and Larson (1995). Following are the conventions used, and examples.

Colons indicate sound stretch:

Esteban: *pers::sonas*

The contents of double parentheses are either description or gestural activity:

Guillermo: ((Shows the students a picture of a volcano from an FMLN *silabario*.))

Double parentheses surrounding two "Xs" indicate unintelligible speach:

Nadia: ((xx))

Single left-handed brackets denote overlapping speech:

Esteban: [así es

Juan: [una

Or overlapping speech and gesture:

Juan: [créditos
                [((Taps twice.))

Equal signs signify closely latched speech:

Daisy: The "h" goes at the beginning of a word, but[=

Ignacio: [but with a "c" you say it[=

Daisy: [=it makes it a "ch"

Rising intonation is noted with an arrow:

Gloria: [e:: ↑
            [((Points at board with ruler.))

Brief pauses are indicated by a period within parentheses:

Fernando: a (.) a (.) a (.) °a°

Or numerically in seconds:

Gloria: [((Brings ruler back to touch chin.))
            [(1.0)

Stress or emphasis in an utterance is underlined:

Juan: in ter es es

Whispered or softly spoken speech is bracketed by degree symbols:

Gloria: °a::°

Examples 13 and 14 have been transcribed in their original Spanish for reasons of analysis. Where appropriate and necessary, English translation has been provided below the original Spanish utterance:

Fernando: *Crédito dice no créditos.*
            Credit it says, not credits.

Appendix B

Example 1
"War is very heavy for us": Giving the Word and the World

1 2 3 4 5 6	Guillermo:	For us, Salvadorans, this word, "war," is very heavy for us. To a Costa Rican, to hear "war" does not cause any effect. In our country, with 12 years of war, it effects us. Because of this war, this conflict, this problem, many of us have had to emigrate. We should know how to write this word.
7	Students:	Yes.
8 9	Guillermo:	It causes, wherever in the world it appears, pain. We had more than 70,000 deaths in our country.
10 11		((He shows the students a picture of a volcano from an FMLN *silabario*[5].))
12 13 14 15 16 17 18 19 20		A *"Guerrero"* is someone who defends territory, or who makes war. But sometimes the words are used wrong, the state discriminates. For example, the word "terrorist." This is someone who causes terror. This can come from the mountains, or from the barracks. And we know that the FMLN wants to win the peace. Now, we're moving forward. In 1971 and 1972, El Salvador was developing. Then the enemies of progress came in and destroyed our country.
21 22	Farabundo :	I have a strange question. Who were the enemies who destroyed our country?
23	Guillermo:	From inside and from without.
24 25 26 27 28 29 30		Let's look at the word "communism." It comes from the word "common," to share things in common. In this way, Salvadorans should be united. Maybe some of you suffered during these times, cutting coffee or something. My brother-in-law was a big owner. The workers worked and cut all day, and the bosses rob you.
31 32	Students:	[(((Are nodding their heads.)) [Yes, yes.

| 33 | Silvia: | I remember working in coffee and working in cotton. |
| 34 | | The bosses always robbed you. |

| 35 | Guillermo: | There are always those who misinterpret about this. |

36		The military leaders—I had one in my family, a very
37		high military official—could do whatever they wanted
38		economically. They could buy and sell cars. They
39		didn't pay taxes. And they could cross the borders as
40		they pleased. But it's not that way anymore. The people
41		are aware and struggling. There are still some abuses, but
42		there are less.

43		Teachers, we can't lie to our students. We have to tell
44		them the truth. About everything. So the government
45		labels us "guerrillas." We told the truth. And that truth
46		hurt the military, the rich.

| 47 | Students: | [((Nod their heads.)) |
| 48 | | [Yes, yes. |

| 49 | Guillermo: | So they killed thousands of teachers. Remember? |

| 50 | Students: | ((Nod their heads.)) |

| 51 | Guillermo: | Because we opened the eyes of the students. |

52		((He relates a story about teaching his students in El
53		Salvador the difference between a "republic" and a
54		"dictatorship," labeling the government of El Salvador
55		a "dictatorship."))

56		This is what I told my students. But the problem was
57		that we had intercoms in our classrooms. And the
58		principal of the school had been listening in on what I
59		had been teaching. She called me in to her office right
60		away. She told me that what I was saying was
61		"inappropriate." And I told her that she ought to get
62		a dictionary and look-up the word 'dictatorship'
63		herself.

64		It's important for you to know this, often we criticize
65		without knowing. So we should know the word
66		"guerra" and the syllable "gue." Monday, we'll write
67		this word, and this syllable, and we'll make a
68		paragraph.

69	A student:	Once the army came and took over our school in
70		El Salvador. They accused us of being "Cubans."
71	Guillermo:	Cuba is a free country.
72		((Elaborates his supportive thoughts on Cuba.))
73	Students:	((Begins to discuss their divergent thoughts on Cuba.))
74	Farabundo:	((To Guillermo:))
75		Then why do so many Cubans come to this country?
76		Cuba is a big country.
77	Students:	[(((Begin to talk about Cuba and the former Soviet Union.))
78	Guillermo:	[We can continue this discussion on Monday. It's late,
79		and class is over for the evening.
80	Students:	((Pack up and leave.))

Appendix C

Example 2
Resisting the Dictation

1	Guillermo:	Now I'll dictate to you. Write "dictation."
2		((He dictates the following:))

3   *"En otoño sopla el viento y los árboles en la plaza*
4   *se quedan sin hojas."*
5   "In autumn, the wind blows and the trees in the plaza
6   are left without leaves."

7	Ana:	((Writes:))

8   *En otoño sopla el viento y los árboles*
9   *en la plaza, se quedan sin hojas.*
10   "In autumn, the wind blows and the trees
11   in the plaza are left without leaves."

12	Farabundo:	((Begins writing down what Guillermo has dictated,
13		appears to become frustrated, stops, and starts
14		sharpening his pencil intently, never getting back
15		to the assignment.))

	Benita/	
16	Ignacio:	((Continue with their individual assignments, and do
17		not participate in the dictation.))

Appendix D

Example 3
   "Some students are not serious": Passive Resistance and Subtle
"Discipline"

1	Farabundo:	((Leaves early, at 8:55.))
2	Guillermo:	Can I make you some homework?
3	Farabundo:	No.
4	Ignacio:	((Packs his things, and silently follows his
5		brother Farabundo. Does not ask for homework.))
6	Guillermo:	((To Ana, Benita—the remaining students
7		—and myself:))
8		Some students are not serious. They don't want
9		to do homework. They think I'm mean, too
10		demanding. They eventually leave the class.

Appendix E

Example 5
Day of the "Apostle"

1   Toward the end of this day's thirty minutes of instruction—the classes
2   normally last two hours—many people, including the students who meet in
3   the other storefront, begin to fill the large common room. Lots of good smelling,
4   homemade dishes covered with tinfoil and wrapped in plastic bags, and
5   bottles of orange, brown and light green soda, start to fill two tables that
6   have been pushed together at the front of the room. The students' families and
7   friends have also come tonight. There are many new faces. As it turns out, the
8   Salvadoran "Day of the Teacher" was yesterday. So this evening, a collective
9   party for all five classes is planned instead of holding regular meetings, in
10   honor of the program's teachers: Guillermo, Nadia, Oscar, Rubén and
11   Cristina. This is an unexpected surprise for the teachers. They didn't know
12   that their students had been planning this for them. There are approximately
13   50-60 people in attendance. The teachers and the program coordinator are
14   asked to sit in front of the assembled group, overlooking the food, in a place
15   of honor. At the insistence of the student organizers, and over my protests, I
16   am also asked to sit with the other teachers up in front, even though I am not a
17   teacher for *Siempre Adelante*. They say, "That doesn't matter, you are a
18   teacher." (They know I work down the street at the neighborhood school.) I
19   join the others. Rosa, a heavyset woman in her late 50s from Rubén's ESL
20   class, who is known as an activist among her classmates, shares her thoughts
21   and gives a "testimonial" on this Day of the Teacher. She says she has known
22   Guillermo for 10 years, ever since he taught her daughter back in El Salvador
23   at his school, before they all came into exile here in the United States. She
24   praises her teacher Rubén, Guillermo, the other teachers with the program,
25   and Daisy, the program coordinator. She says she has learned much from her
26   teacher, has much respect for teachers in general, and for all the important
27   work that they do. She refers to teachers as "apostles of literacy," and
28   "warriors against ignorance." The assembled crowd of now 80 people
29   vocalizes its agreement. There are several other student "testimonials"—by
30   the other event organizers, and by whomever is moved to speak from the
31   audience. The teachers are then given wrapped presents. As they open them,
32   the crowd of students and well-wishers is excited for and with them. The
33   party continues with plates of food being given to each teacher (including
34   myself), and then to the rest of the crowd. Later, after the food, there is music
35   and dancing.

Appendix F

Example 6
  "Through dictation and memorizing words": An Interview with Students

1   Marc: How do adults best learn to read and write?

2   Juan: It has to do with the attitude of the student, if they pay
3   attention. And also the intelligence of the teacher.

4   Samuel: By reviewing a board full of words.

5   Veronica: Through dictation and memorizing words.

6   Esteban: Letters. Syllables.

7   Gloria: The Sir puts words on the board, explains how to read them,
8   and reviews them.

9   Marc: What is the role of the teacher, and of the student, in this
10   process?

11 Juan: The teacher has to say what is right and what is wrong.
12   The student has to pay attention.

13 Marc: Have you improved your literacy? Are you making progress?

14 Veronica: You have to have a lot of persistence. I say it's good.

15 Juan: The teacher knows what one can do.

16 Esteban: I was seeing in Mr. Linares that we weren't advancing quickly,
17   or well.

18 Veronica: No. He said that it was a problem of people not coming.

Appendix G

Example 7
War, Part II

1	Daisy:	Using your ideas, how could we extend this sentence?
2	Farabundo:	*La guerra no es buena porque*
3		*ha destruido mucho el país.*
4		War is bad because it has
5		destroyed the country much.
6	Daisy:	((Changes the sentence to read:))
7		*La guerra no es buena porque*
8		*ha destruido mucho el país.*
9		War is bad because it has
10		destroyed the country much.
11		This sentence tells me much more.
12	Gloria:	Let's put "El Salvador."
13	Daisy:	Where should I put it?
14	Farabundo:	*"La guerra de El Salvador no es buena porque*
15		*ha destruido mucho el país,"* o
16		*"La guerra no es buena porque*
17		*ha destruido mucho el país de El Salvador."*
18		"The war of EL *Salvador* is not good
19		because it has destroyed the country much," or
20		"The war is not good because it has
21		destroyed the country of El Salvador much."
22	Daisy:	((Changes the sentence to read:))
23		*La guerra de El Salvador no es buena porque*
24		*ha destruido mucho el país.*
25		The war of EL Salvador is not good
26		because it has destroyed the country much.
27		*La guerra de El Salvador no es buena porque*
28		*ha destruido mucho el país.*
29		The war of EL Salvador is not good because
30		it has destroyed the country much.

31	Daisy:	Which sentence conveys more meaning
32		and information?

33	Farabundo:	With the first version, I didn't know what part
34		of the world it pertained to.

35	Gloria:	The last version is more complex.

36	Daisy:	(xx) because (xx) there is a reason.
37		We could talk for months on this reality.

38	Students:	((Begin to share personal stories about their
39		experiences with the war in El Salvador.))

40	Gloria:	We were out in a car. With my sister. I was eight.
41		The soldiers threw a bomb at the car.
42		All the people died, including four children.
43		They took me to the hospital. I still have this mark here.

44		((She indicates a scar on her head
45		just above the hair line.))
46		I was all bloody on my face. My sister lived.
47		The driver was yelling at the soldiers,
48		"Don't throw bombs at me! I'm...(xx)...(xx)..."
49		But they did it anyway.

50	Students:	((Talk about the death squads, the differences
51		between the FMLN and the Salvadoran government,
52		and the military's practice of "forced conscription."))

53	Gloria:	It's getting worse again. Everyone is armed.

54	Daisy:	People have had to re-arm to protect themselves.
55		There are on-going skirmishes, even though
56		the elections are approaching.

57		There are personal stories, but I think we have to look
58		at larger processes. Before the semester is over, we're
59		going to get an update from *Siempre* on the Salvadoran
60		situation. Using your ideas, and discussion, we're going
61		to develop this.

62		((Referring to the sentence they wrote about war
63		in El Salvador:))

64		We're going to talk more about this,

65   and extend the paragraph.

66 Samuel: My brothers, cousins, were all on the left.
67   They're all finished now.

Appendix H

Example 8
  A Geo-political Text

Los paises del 3<u>er</u> mundo nunca se van a superar porque este país no los deja. La guerra en El Salvador es un ejemplo de eso. La pobreza de ese país es causada por los EEUU. Los EEUU sabe que con México tiene el futuro, por eso quiere el tratado de libre comercio. México tampoco se supera, este país impide la posibilidad de progreso a otros países. Un ejército nunca puede (XX) con la organización de un pueblo.

The countries of the 3rd World are never going to advance, because this country will not let them. The war in El Salvador is an example of this. The poverty of this country is caused by the United States. The United States knows that it has a future with Mexico, therefore it wants NAFTA. Mexico is not improving either, this country impedes the possibility for progress of other countries. An army can never (xx) against the organization of the people.

Appendix I

Example 9

Fill in the Blank

1 2	Gloria:	[(((Is holding a piece of paper with "gui" printed on it up to one of the blank spaces on the board.))
3		[I put it here?
4 5	Samuel:	No. Where it says "Guillermo." There. There above. That part there.
6	Esteban:	Yes.
7 8	Gloria:	((She tapes the card with its mate on the board, creating "Guillermo."))
9	Samuel:	[(((To Gloria and Daisy:))
10		[You have to use a capital letter with names.
11	Daisy:	You're right. Next time, I'll correct it.
12	Farabundo:	Does it say *"cajita"* there?
13 14	Daisy:	Very good. I was thinking *"cajeta,"* a sweet. But very good. That's good.
15	Esteban:	((Makes the word: jigante.))
16	Esteban:	How's this?
17	Daisy:	What's your opinion?
18	Gloria:	It goes with the "j."
19	Samuel:	With the "g."
20	Esteban:	With the "j."
21	Gloria:	[(((To Daisy, in the informal *tú* form:))
22		[Daisy, will you do me a favor?
23	Daisy:	Yes. What?

24	Gloria:	Will you let me copy the words into my notebook?
25	Students:	((Laugh because they know of Daisy's preference not
26		to have her students copy from the board.))
27	Daisy:	Yes.
28		But first let's read them.

Appendix J

Example 10
Words that Begin with "H"

| 1
2 | Daisy: | How do we know when to put an "h"?
Let's get more examples. |

3 Ignacio: [(((Holds up the *Silabario Hispano Americano*))

4 [There are lots of examples in this book.

5 Daisy: Oh, good.

6 But let's come up with examples ourselves.

7 ((She writes on board:))

8 [*helados / elados*

9 Ignacio: [(((Reads as Daisy writes this
10 on the board.))

11 Daisy: Silvia, how do we know? Can we?

12 We can't. There is no way. We just have to
13 learn the words ((([that begin with the silent "h"]))).

14 Like Ignacio said, the only way to know them is to
15 read them.

16 When the "h" is in the middle of a word,
17 the "c" takes it up.

18 Daisy: And what does that make?

19 Ignacio: The "ch."

20 Daisy: Let me sum-up what you said, Ignacio.
21 And tell me if I'm wrong.

22 The "h" goes at the beginning of a word,
23 but[=

24 Ignacio: [but with a "c" you say it[=

25 Daisy: [=it makes it a "ch"

26 Ignacio: But if it's in a proper name, you don't pronounce the "h."

Appendix K

Example 11

"During dictation, well, one learns the words": An Interview with Students

1 2	Gregorio:	Do you think you've learned during your time in this course? Or is the rhythm too slow for you?
3 4	Patricia:	It's slow, but we're advancing. It's not the instructors' fault.
5		[It's because of this head I have, you know.
6		[(((She raps her closed fist three times on her head.))
7 8	Gregorio:	What are your favorite exercises? What helps you learn the best?
9	Fernando:	Dictation.
10	Esteban:	Dictation.
11	Veronica:	During dictation, well, one learns the words.
12 13	Fernando:	When the teacher writes on the board, one loses their fear.
14	Gregorio:	The theme, the word discussion, does it help? Is it important?
15 16 17 18	Esteban:	Well, you know, sometimes we spend 40 minutes —half the time [discussing the theme]. Maybe we could be learning other things. We could talk about the word more quickly.
19 20	Carlos:	The teacher should say what the word is. But that's it.

Appendix L

Example 12
 The "Cooperative" Text

> *coopera Tiva de ahorro y CrédiTo.*
> Savings and Credit Cooperative

EsTa es una agrupación de personas que se unen para ahorrar dinero y proporcionarse crédito a intereses razonables.

This is a group of people who unite to save money and offer credit at reasonable rates.

los miembros (socios) de esTa cooperaTiva de ahorro adquienen el hábito de ahorrar y se ayudan entre ellos mismos para resoluer problemas económicos.

The members of this savings cooperative become accustomed to the habit of saving, and they help each other resolve economic problems.

Esta cooperativa tiene el beneficio de presTar dineros con menos requisitos de los que piden un <u>Banco</u> y a un interés más baJo que el de los presTamisTas.

This cooperative has the benefit of being able to loan money with less requirements than a bank asks for, and at a lower interest than that of those who regularly loan money.

Appendix M

Example 13

"Crédito dice, no créditos": Assisting Juan

| 1 | Juan: | ((Gets up, waits, and then begins to read |
| 2 | | from the board.)) |

| 3 | | [*°co°*= |
| 4 | | [((Taps board under syllable with ruler.)) |

| | Nadia/ | |
| 5 | Gloria: | *[(xx)* |

| 6 | Juan: | *[=co* |
| 7 | | [((Taps.)) |

| 8 | Nadia: | ((To Gloria:)) |

| 9 | | *A bueno (xx).* |
| 10 | | Oh fine (xx). |

| 11 | Juan: | *[per   -   [a* |
| 12 | | [((Taps.))   [((Taps.)) |

| 13 | | *[tiva* |
| 14 | | [((Taps.)) |

| 15 | | *[de* |
| 16 | | [((Taps.)) |

17		*[a*
18		[((Taps, lifts ruler, and pauses, moving the ruler
19		back and forth under *"horros,"* touching
20		the board once.))

| 21 | | ((Long pause.)) |

| 22 | | *[horros=* |

| 23 | | [((Taps.)) |

| 24 | Nadia: | Un huh. |

| 25 | Esteban: | *[Ahorro* |

| 26 | Juan: | [=*y* |
| 27 | | [((Taps.)) |

| 28 | | [*créditos* |
| 29 | | [((T̄aps twice.)) |

30		[*Allí*
31		[There
32		[((Indicating his is finished reading that part.))

| 33 | Fernando: | *Crédito dice n[o créditos.* |
| 34 | | Credit it says no[t credits. |

| 35 | Gloria: | [*crédito* |

| 36 | | ((Laughs.)) |

| 37 | Juan: | ((Looks back at the word "*crédito*," and brings |
| 38 | | his hand with the ruler near his mouth, pensive.)) |

39	Fernando:	*crédito - llevara la* "s"
40		credit - ((as if)) it took the "s"
41		((or))
42		credit - ((as if)) he took the "s" to it

| 43 | Juan: | *Créditos (xx)* |

| 44 | Fernando: | *Cr̄édito* |

45	Juan:	*Pero (xx) la* "s" *que ya no [tenía*
46		But (xx) the "s" that it didn't alr[eady have
47		((or))
48		But (xx) the "s" that I didn't alr[eady have
49		[((Begins to grin.))

| 50 | All: | ((Begin to laugh.)) |

| 51 | Juan: | ((Juan's grin turns into a big smile |
| 52 | | as he too begins to laugh.)) |

| 53 | All: | ((All laugh heartily.)) |

54	Esteban:	[*Cuando la lleva ¿no?*
55		[When he brought it—right?
56		((or))
57		[When it was brought—right?

58 All: [((Are still laughing.))

59 Gloria: *Hay no la "s" que ya no tenga y se no [(xx)]*
60   ((not translatable))

61 Juan: [(*xx]*
62   *Pero que la tenemos en [mente y=*
63   but we have it in our [mind and=

64   [((Pointing toward his
65   head with the ruler.))

66 Nadia: [*Va::*
67   [Go ahead

68   ((Chuckles.))

69 Juan: =[(xx)
70   [((pointing toward the board))

71   ((Juan goes on to read the rest of the text.))

Appendix N

Example 14
Juan and Esteban Assist Gloria

1	Gloria:	[e::↑
2		[((Points at board with ruler.))
3		[((Brings ruler back to touch chin.))
4		[(1.0)
5	Juan:	<u>es</u>ta
6	Gloria:	*e*
7		*es:: ta*
8		(1.5)
9	Esteban:	*es*
10	Gloria:	*es*
11	Esteban:	*u[na*
12	Juan:	[*una*
13	Gloria:	*una*
14		(0.8)
15	Esteban:	*a*
16	Gloria:	((Opens mouth as if to make the sound "ah."))
17		°*a::*°
18	Esteban:	*gru [pa ción*
19	Juan:	[*gru pa ción (.) ci[ón*
20	Gloria:	[*grupacióne*
21	Juan/	
	Esteban:	*grupación*
22	Gloria:	[*grupación*
23		[((Taps ruler on the board twice as
24		she reads "*grupación*."))

25	Gloria:	*[d[e*
26		[((Taps.))
27	Juan:	*[de*
28	Gloria:	[((Is looking intently at the word on the board.))
29		[((Taps ruler under the "p" of "*personas.*"))
30		[(1.0)
31	Juan:	*Yo no miro por sentar (xx)*
32		I can't see because of sitting (xx)
33	Esteban:	*pers::*
34	Gloria:	*[pers:sonal*
35		[((Taps twice.))
36	Esteban:	*pers::sonas*
37	Juan:	*de personas*
38	Gloria:	*[pe son as::s*
39		[((Taps twice.))
40	Juan:	*sonas*
41	Gloria:	((Laughs.))
42	Juan:	*personas*

MARC PRUYN

Appendix O

Example 15
Juan, Esteban and Gloria Assist Fernando

1   Fernando: *pro por cionar se*

2   (0.2)

3   *cré crédito*
4   *y*

5   *a̲ (.) a (.) a (.) °a°*

6   Juan: *i[n ter es̲ es*

7   Esteban: *[°in ter e°*

8   Fernando: (0.4)

9   *a intereses*

10 Esteban: *°a°*

11 Fernando: *ra zones*

12 Esteban: *razonables*

13 Fernando: *ra ra [ra razonables*

14 Gloria: *[ra zonables̲*

15 Esteban: *[razonables*

16 Fernando: *[razonables*

17   *(xx)*

18 All: ((Give Fernando an applause.))

References

Atkinson, G. and Heritage, J. 1984. *Structures of Social Action: Studies of Conversation Analysis.* Cambridge: Cambridge University Press.

Larson, J. 1995. *Talk Matters: Knowledge Distribution Among Novice Writers in Kindergarten.* An unpublished dissertation. University of California, Los Angeles.

Index